UNDEFEATED

Stories of Survival, Resilience
and Relevance in Salem, Oregon

Printed in the United States of America

TABLE OF CONTENTS

	DEDICATION	9
	ACKNOWLEDGEMENTS	11
	INTRODUCTION	15
1	THE FLOOD	17
2	THE FACE IN THE MIRROR	45
3	A DOSE OF GOOD MEDICINE	67
4	LIKE A ROCK	97
5	FIGHTING	127
6	THE STENCH	151
7	LOSING THE FIGHT, WINNING THE BATTLE	167
	CONCLUSION	193

DEDICATION

This book is dedicated to those who have ever felt like giving up. Those who have experienced circumstances in life that have left them feeling hopeless and defeated. Those who feel tormented by past mistakes and failures. Those who are suffering from life-destroying addictions and habits. If you need HOPE, and desire to overcome and live a life that is UNDEFEATED by these issues, then this book is for you!

ACKNOWLEDGEMENTS

I would like to thank Kevin Reich for his vision for this book and Julie Pilgrim for her hard work in making it a reality. And to the people of Relevant Life, thank you for your boldness and vulnerability in sharing your personal stories.

This book would not have been published without the amazing efforts of our project manager and editor, Hayley Pandolph. Her untiring resolve pushed this project forward and turned it into a stunning victory. Thank you for your great fortitude and diligence. Deep thanks to our incredible Editor in Chief, Michelle Cuthrell, and Executive Editor, Nicole Phinney Lowell, for all the amazing work they do. I would also like to thank our invaluable proofreader, Melody Davis, for the focus and energy she has put into perfecting our words.

Lastly, I want to extend our gratitude to the creative and very talented Ann Clayton, who designed the beautiful cover for *Undefeated: Stories of Survival, Resilience and Relevance in Salem, Oregon.*

Daren Lindley
President and CEO
Good Catch Publishing

The book you are about to read
is a compilation of authentic life stories.
The facts are true, and the events are real.
These storytellers have dealt with crisis, tragedy, abuse
and neglect and have shared their most private moments,
mess-ups and hang-ups in order for others to learn and
grow from them. In order to protect the identities of those
involved in their pasts, the names and details of some
storytellers have been withheld or changed.

INTRODUCTION

Defeated or UNDEFEATED? Will the circumstances of your life bring about a win or a loss? What do you do when life is careening out of control? What if addiction has overtaken you or abuse chained you with fear? Is depression escapable? Can you ever get beyond your past mistakes? Will relationships ever be healthy again? Are you destined to be held captive by old habits and thought patterns? Do miracles really happen?

These are some of the questions that others have asked and found answers to. Bottom line, you want to know … can my life really change?

Your life really can change! It is possible to become a new person. The seven stories you are about to read prove positively that people right here in Salem, Oregon, have stopped dying and started living. Whether they've experienced abuse, broken promises, shattered dreams or suffocating addictions, the resounding answer is, "Yes! You can live UNDEFEATED and come out experiencing freedom on the other side." The potential for a bright future awaits you.

Expect inspiration, hope and transformation! As you walk with each real person through the pages of this book, you will not only find riveting accounts of their hardships, but you will also learn the secrets that brought about their breakthroughs. These people are no longer living in the

UNDEFEATED

shadows of yesterday; they are thriving with a sense of undertaking and purpose TODAY. May these stories inspire you to do the same!

THE FLOOD
The Story of Randy and Cheryl
Written by Marty Minchin

Midnight was closing in, but I kept walking.

I headed out along a sidewalk in the pitch-black night, continuing on even when it led into seedier and seedier neighborhoods.

I walked in a straight line through Modesto, not caring about my surroundings. After years of meth addiction, I knew these places well.

Our camper and most of our possessions were filled with mud and water after the severe flooding in the San Joaquin Valley a few weeks before. My girlfriend, Cheryl, and I had since lost our jobs and our car and had gotten pneumonia. We had broken down crying in front of FEMA representatives, and earlier that day Cheryl and I had fought for the first time in our two-year relationship. She was all I had to hold on to, and now I might be losing her, too.

Before the floods, we had lived in a nest of meth use. We were longtime addicts, and practically everyone we knew cooked, used or sold drugs, too. Now, we had nothing. Our only way out of Modesto would be in my old pickup truck, but it was sitting at the bottom of a flooded river miles away. I paused on the sidewalk and looked up into the night sky. Was anyone up there?

If I get my truck back, I will get my family out of here.
That wasn't all I had to offer.
I will never touch drugs again.

ตตต

My life got off to a good start. My siblings and I were close, and I had a happy childhood. Through my school years I didn't drink or do drugs; I was generally a responsible, upbeat young man.

By high school, I was head over heels in love with my classmate Janet. We got engaged after I graduated and got a job with an asphalt paving company. Our wedding day was set for two months after she finished her senior year. We had booked the church and the preacher; she had bought her dress. We had a peaceful, loving relationship, and anything she wanted, I gave her.

When I came home from work one Friday to the apartment we shared, she was sitting on the couch waiting for me. She skipped pleasantries that summer day.

"I'm going to see my mom." Her mother lived in Oroville, California, several hours away, and it wasn't unusual for Janet to visit her.

"How long are you going to stay?"

The silence before she answered got my attention. This wasn't the casual conversation I thought it was.

"Randy, I'm moving home."

She slid her engagement ring off her finger and laid it in my palm.

THE FLOOD

I was still staring at it in shock when she breezed out the door for the last time.

გადადადა

Janet never explained why she broke up with me, and I was devastated. After she left, nothing seemed to matter anymore, and I stopped eating and sleeping. It was hard to concentrate on daily life. I'd rather have played on a busy freeway than endure the pain of her leaving, so that's exactly what I did.

I started driving trucks when I was 16. The flat terrain in Northern California is prime for agriculture, and the fields are filled with fruit and nut trees and endless rows of vegetables. Trucks transport the produce to wineries, canneries and packaging plants, and truck drivers were in high demand.

After classes in high school, I'd work late into the night driving loads of produce to their destinations and then get up for school the next morning. By the time I was 18, I was running loads to Los Angeles and back by myself. When grapes, tomatoes and peaches came in season in the summer, we would haul loads around the clock. Every time we returned to the farm another load was ready to go. We were paid by the trip, so the more I drove the more money I earned.

Sleep was a nuisance; it detracted from the time I could drive and earn money. In the late 1970s, the State of California had few regulations on truckers' hours, so we drove as much as we could to maximize our paychecks. I labored to stay awake on trips, sometimes driving 100 miles and not remembering an inch of it. Sometimes I'd nod off and wake up when the truck ran off the side of the road.

My truck once jumped a curb while I was asleep at the wheel. I'd startle awake and find my truck driving into oncoming traffic with another truck barreling toward me at full speed. So many times, I'd look over into the empty passenger seat after a close call and ask why I was still alive.

I stayed connected with other truckers over the CB radios. Many of them had been driving for years, and they knew the secret to staying awake.

The first time I tried meth, it was great. I made a long haul and didn't bat an eyelid. I kept my meth use under control for a while, just using enough to get me there and back on a haul and then I'd stop until the next trip. Meth made me invincible. In November of 1979, I drove 22,000 miles in 25 days. I lost 33 pounds because I only stopped for fuel and to load and unload my truck.

But meth use creeps up on you. No one sets out to become an addict. My work drug use spilled over into the weekends, and before long I was using it socially. All of my lines became blurred.

❧❧❧

THE FLOOD

I married Michelle in 1982 and introduced her to meth. I was 23 years old, and when we met, I wondered why she had been married four times before. But love prevailed, and I proposed. Our daughter was born the next year, but by 1984 I wanted out of the marriage. I stayed because of our daughter, however, and soon we had a son. Michelle and I were miserable together, and I began to take every load I could to avoid going home.

My routine started on Sunday night, when I'd take off for a week of runs from Turlock, California, to Los Angeles and the Bay area. I'd drag myself home on Saturday morning after a week without sleep. If I stayed, I'd sleep until Sunday afternoon, grab some clean clothes and leave again. If I wasn't working or sleeping, I'd get wired on meth and leave for the night. Often I wouldn't return for two weeks.

Michelle could be irrational and hostile, especially when she got angry. Anything was justifiable in her mind.

One afternoon I headed out to leave in my little blue Ford Pinto, and she knew if I got in the car I probably wouldn't come back for weeks.

She followed me to the driveway waving my Ruger 357 Magnum, which I'd seen her do before. This time she shot out the front tire before I could slide into the driver's seat.

"Are you crazy?" I shouted. The look in her eyes was all the answer I needed.

She pulled the hammer back and pointed the gun at me, shaking her finger on the other hand. I wanted to choke her, but there was a gun between us.

"Are you going to shoot me, too?"

I'd let her decide. I turned my back and walked away, and she pulled the trigger.

I started running.

My breathing was too heavy for me to hear the bullets whistling by, but I ran through a field strewn with clods of dirt, hoping that her aim was off. She emptied the gun while I ran, and I stopped only when I got out of range, heaving from the sprint. Only then was it safe for me to head over to my mom's and call the sheriff.

ॐॐॐ

No matter how bad things got with Michelle or how many times I packed up my things to leave her for good, I kept going back because of my kids. I felt like that was the thing to do, even though all the kids saw was their mother and me acting hateful toward each other. Our battles raged on.

By 1988, the year my beloved dad died, my life was completely out of control. I had become a full-blown meth addict. I rarely kept a job for long. I used and sold drugs, and to earn extra money, I also sold stolen diesel fuel, trucks and trailers. A gun was always tucked in my belt, as I hung out with a crowd that was into almost everything.

One evening as I smoked meth in my friend Nate's bedroom, I surveyed the crew hanging around the edges of the room pulling on their glass pipes. If you sat in a poker game with these guys, you'd want to keep your hand on your gun. One guy had a drug lab. Another was trying to make a deal with a paper bag of counterfeit money. Nate and I discussed the possibility of selling a batch of stolen diesel fuel together.

"Do you have your 45 with you?" he asked.

I pulled it out of my belt to show him. He seemed fascinated with the weapon.

"Is it loud?"

"Shoot it. You'll find out."

"That's okay."

I rolled the gun over in my hand.

"Is it loud?" Nate asked again.

"I suppose it is."

"How loud?"

I was tired of the questions. I pulled the trigger and shot a hole in the floor at the foot of Nate's bed.

The guys plastered themselves to the wall, looking like they'd just seen something from a horror movie. The ones who knew about the explosives under the house stared at me, bug-eyed.

Nate finally broke the long silence.

"Hey. You just shot a hole in the floor."

"Take it easy." I grabbed a screwdriver off his dresser and jammed it in the hole. "There. I fixed it."

An uneasy round of chuckles followed, and we went back to our pipes. Nate's wife, who he'd locked out of the bedroom while we smoked, was hanging out in the living room but didn't say a word about the gunshot.

One of those guys was found a few weeks later floating

in a canal with a screwdriver in his head. When you're immersed in a world of drug addicts, no one has the capability to help anyone else out of it. We were like cows wandering through a pasture with no way through the fence. For us, there was no hope, no light at the end of the tunnel.

≈≈≈

"Hey, have you met Jack?" The girl I was getting wired with that night kept asking. "You have to meet him. He's such a neat guy."

Happy Jack, as he was known, was a chef, a guy who cooked meth. He was well loved in the drug community for his fun personality.

However great Happy Jack was, the last thing I needed was another friend in the drug business.

"Just give me a ride to the house, then," Vera pleaded. "You'll meet him there."

"I'll stay in the car while you talk to him."

Vera was only in the house for a minute before she bounded back to the driveway.

"C'mon. He wants to meet you."

I reluctantly followed her into the garage, but instantly regretted not meeting Happy Jack sooner. Within minutes, I knew Jack and I would be lifelong friends. We settled into his room, a converted garage, and smoked some meth.

Minutes later, Jack's sister Cheryl, a cute blonde

wearing blue jeans and cowboy boots, strode confidently in the door after an evening of country line dancing at a bar. She threw herself down on Jack's bed, her long hair brushing past her shoulders, and motioned toward me.

"Who's Dimples?"

I blushed.

As soon as Cheryl and I started talking, the other people in the room faded away. We walked through the house to Cheryl's room, and with help from all of the meth in our systems, we stayed up talking for 12 hours. We shared our dreams and our outlooks on life. It was such a welcome relief to talk with someone who actually considered the words that came out of my mouth. She was intelligent and had opinions, and she listened to mine with interest.

Cheryl left me with an observation.

"You're a prince who thinks he's a frog."

અન્ય અન્ય

Michelle and I were still married, so I didn't initially follow up with Cheryl after our night-long talk. But I ran into Jack occasionally with mutual friends.

"You really need to come by the house," he would say, without adding a reason. "I mean it. You should come over to the house."

I was getting the same message from Vera. Cheryl was putting full-court pressure on her and Jack to get me back to the house.

UNDEFEATED

Thirty days after we first met and two days after Cheryl's 36th birthday, I stopped by. It was 1995, and we have been together ever since.

Even though we were both meth addicts, Cheryl and I had been through enough relationship troubles to want ground rules for this one.

One of our first prohibitions was against yelling. I was leaving a relationship characterized by yelling, and Cheryl felt like she'd had 100 relationships like that. We agreed not to yell at each other, at our kids or at anybody else. It made the relationship comfortable and even healthy.

Something calmed down in me when I met Cheryl. In a way, our relationship was the beginning of a new life for me, and I began to disentangle myself from some of my illegal activities. But we were still meth addicts and suffered the consequences of addiction.

Over the next two years, we were homeless at times and once lived in a broken-down van in Cheryl's parents' driveway. We camped out in an abandoned house. Other times, we couch-hopped between friends' and relatives' houses.

A guy who wanted Jack to cook meth for him set Jack up in a good-sized trailer on several hundred acres in the country outside Modesto. The property was expansive, and we soon joined Jack and several other family members on the land. We set up a cozy one-bedroom camper trailer. I drove a truck, and Cheryl worked at Subway. We often talked about how we were better than other drug addicts because we didn't steal from our friends or try to hurt people. We worked hard for a living, and we wondered why bad things kept happening to us.

෨෨෨

We sat out in the cold air on New Year's Eve in 1996, savoring the quiet evening and our visit with Cheryl's kids. Our camper was half a mile from the San Joaquin River, but around 11 p.m., we heard the gurgling of running water much closer.

That winter brought a weather phenomenon called the pineapple express, a series of warm tropical storms to the West Coast that dropped heavy rains through December. The rivers were full, and dams were being opened to release the burgeoning waters. The excess poured into the San Joaquin River, and that night it jumped the banks on our property.

"Something's wrong," Cheryl told me. "I have a bad feeling about the water."

She found a flashlight and shined it toward the gully just below our camper. Normally dry, it was now filling with river water.

We leapt up in a panic.

"The car!" I pointed to Cheryl's Datsun, the only working vehicle we had. We knew there were some low spots between our camper and the road, so we hooked the car to a bucket loader that was parked on the property and pulled it to higher ground. The next morning the water was ankle-deep with no signs of slowing, so we hustled

Cheryl's elderly dad and the kids, who also lived with us in our compound, through the neighbor's property and into town, where we distributed them to family members around Modesto. Now only Jack and his wife were left.

At about 6 p.m. New Year's Day, we drove back to the property to get them. The water was now knee-deep, and we had to stop several miles from their trailer.

"We need to get out of here in a couple of hours," we called to Jack and Ellen before ducking into a camper to save what we could. We piled pictures and electronics on shelves, moving what we could off the floor in case the water flooded the camper. Cheryl pulled out our backpacks, which we stuffed with clothes and personal hygiene items.

We had no food, water or electricity in the trailers. We were terrified, but if we died trying to evacuate, at least we would have tried to save ourselves.

The water was waist-high when the four of us gathered for the hike out. It was midnight, and the swirling water was strong and frightening, a force that could carry us away if we lost our footing.

I led our little caravan over terrain that was now unfamiliar. The murky water hid the gopher holes and barbed-wire fences we knew were there. We hoped that the downed power lines around us weren't live.

The trek was slow. We walked single-file in a compact line so that we could snatch anyone who fell out of the freezing current. Our flashlights bounced off the black water, giving no indication of what was underneath.

THE FLOOD

We waded out of the flood around 2 a.m., thankful that we were alive. Behind us, our home and possessions were likely underwater. We had no idea what lay ahead of us.

෨෨෨

The flood was only the beginning of the devastation in our lives.

When I tried driving Cheryl's car through some standing water to get to my boss' place, the water ruined the motor, and we lost the car. Cheryl couldn't get to work, so she lost her job. My pickup truck was sitting in a flooded river 15 miles away. The IRS had seized my boss' business, so I was out of work, too.

In hopes of salvaging some of our possessions, we rowed an aluminum boat to our camper. When we docked the boat at the edge of the floodwaters, we found ice on the bottom. We saved a few things, but we had nowhere to take them so we set up camp where our boat landed so that we could guard our stuff.

A FEMA team patrolling the flood may have saved our lives. When they drove up, we hadn't had anything to drink or eat in about a day, and we were freezing. The two FEMA officials invited us to sit in the back of their car to warm up, and they handed us bottles of water and some food. We cried like babies, so thankful for their kindness.

They drove Cheryl to her son's house in Modesto. I wanted to stay behind with our stuff, so the guys left me with a bottle of water and a burrito. Cheryl picked me up later that day, and in our physical and emotional exhaustion, we got into the first real fight of our two-year relationship. My spirits sagged; my relationship with Cheryl was the only thing I had left for support. I had nowhere to turn.

When the night had settled in, I slipped out the front door for a walk. I had nothing and no one to turn to for help anymore. I glanced at the night sky. Help would have to come from above. If God would restore my pickup truck, I promised, we'd leave town and be done with drugs forever.

৵৵৵

We were at a turning point.

Cheryl and I could struggle back into our lives of addiction in Modesto. FEMA would give us a little money, and we could use that to rent an apartment in town and look for new jobs. I knew, however, that would lead us right back into our old rut.

The other option was to leave town. On a recent job hauling hay out of Nevada, I had seen expanses of irrigated valleys in the middle of nowhere.

"If we're going to change our lives, we have to change our environment," I told Cheryl, who burst into tears at the idea. "But you and I have to leave by ourselves."

"But, the kids, my mom …" We both were sick at the idea of leaving our loved ones behind. But a new start meant that we had to be surrounded by a new location and new people. I felt so strongly about moving that I would have lied to Cheryl to get her to leave. But I didn't have to.

"If we leave, within a year they will all follow us," I told her. "I know this like I know the sun's coming up tomorrow. Trust me on this."

Now, we just had to find a way out of town, which could be complicated. The only vehicle we owned was full of mud and river water somewhere on my boss' property. It probably needed an engine, and the tags were expired. Neither of us had a license.

☙☙☙

"Stop!" I screamed at Betty, Cheryl's mother. Out of the corner of my eye I had glimpsed a beat-up brown truck parked on the edge of the two-lane highway we were traveling.

Could it be?

"That's my truck. I know it is."

Betty pulled over, but she wasn't convinced. We stared out the back window of her car.

"Turn around. That's it." I couldn't believe what I was seeing. That was my 1967 Chevy long-bed pickup, which I'd traded one-sixteenth of an ounce of meth for 10 years ago.

"Are you sure that's your truck? I thought it was stuck in the mud on a river bottom."

"Does a mama know her baby?"

UNDEFEATED

Betty turned the car around and pulled into the gravel parking lot in front of Country Diner, which shined like a beacon when the afternoon sun hit it the right way. If the truck had been parked properly in the parking lot, I never would have seen it. But here it was, on the side of the road, like it was waiting for me.

The parking lot was deserted, so Betty and I peered in the windows of the truck. The keys were hanging in the ignition, and I opened the door and slid into the familiar driver's seat. The last time I had seen the truck the battery was dead, and it was out of gas. The engine had needed more work than I could afford.

It roared to life when I turned the key.

The pickup's last known whereabouts had been at least six miles away and on the opposite side of the river. The back window was crusted with river mud, and the doors were dented where debris in the flooded river had crashed into it. Someone had stolen the truck, replaced the cracked tires and repaired the engine. All that remained for a successful theft was changing the VIN number.

"I'll see you at home!" I called to Betty before pulling out on the road.

God laid that truck in my hands that day, less than 12 hours after I had sincerely asked him for help. There's no way the money from FEMA would have covered the repairs that truck needed. I had given God a promise that I would change my life in return, and I had no intention of going back on it.

THE FLOOD

⋙⋙⋙

Cheryl and I pulled out of Modesto two weeks later, literally on a prayer.

We still didn't have drivers' licenses, and while I had the papers on the truck, it wasn't registered, and we didn't have insurance. We hooked a tow bar to the old Datsun and pulled it behind the truck in hopes that it would hide the expired tags. We knew getting out of town was the only way we could stop doing drugs.

Cheryl wasn't convinced that God was working in our lives, but she knew how strongly I believed that God had put that pickup on the side of the road. She promised me she wouldn't touch meth again. I could hardly believe it.

We drove toward Reno and stopped at Donner Summit before we crossed into Nevada. This rest stop is particularly scenic and more like a park, with a beautiful view of the Sierra Nevada Mountains. It was time for me to fully dispose of my drug life.

Cheryl wasn't sure what life would be like without drugs, but my determination to move forward overrode any nostalgia I might have had for meth. I pocketed a few baggies of dope I had in the truck, grabbed our last glass pipe and walked with Cheryl to a secluded, wooded area at the rest stop.

I crouched down and emptied the dope onto the ground, then stuffed the empty baggies in my pocket. The last to go was the glass pipe, which I hurled at the pavement.

To our amazement, it didn't break. We stared at each other in wonder. Glass pipes are extremely fragile. Sometimes all it takes is a change in temperature for one to shatter. It was unheard of for one not to shatter on the ground.

"That's weird," I muttered. I picked it up again and threw it back at the ground, harder this time. It bounced.

It's like some nasty presence is here on this mountain with us, wanting us to hang onto that pipe just in case.

This time, I flung the pipe far into the forest. Even if it was still intact after it landed, it was no longer part of my life. My 19 years of drug use were over, and I had taken one more step in keeping my promise to God.

Cheryl and I walked quietly through the parking lot. She knew that I was done with drugs, and if she wanted a life with me, she had to be done, too.

የታየታ

It felt like God was laying out a smooth path for us, even though we hadn't done a doggone thing for him. We settled in Lake Lahontan for six months, where we lived in the campground for free and got jobs helping with flood cleanup — the same flood that devastated our lives in California.

In the few weeks before we started our jobs, we slept and ate a lot, recovering from the trauma of the flood. By the end of our rest period, Cheryl had lost her desire for meth.

THE FLOOD

Because our jobs were at the lake, we didn't have to drive anywhere. We slept in the camper on the back of our truck and cooked over a campfire. Because of the extreme heat in the summer, we often couldn't fall asleep until late at night when the air cooled. In the evening hours, Cheryl would read to me. That's when we really began to get to know each other.

In 2002, we moved to Oregon, and Betty followed us there a few years later. We had jobs and money to take care of ourselves and help our children. In our minds, we were prospering.

Betty was diagnosed with lung cancer at the end of 2008, and a few days before Labor Day 2009, she was nearing death. Cheryl stayed with her as much as she could, comforting Betty through the pain. One day Betty tried to sit up, but she couldn't. Cheryl and her nephew carried Betty to bed and gave her morphine, and Betty lapsed into unconsciousness.

Cheryl sat with her all night, holding her hand. I found her scared and exhausted the next morning. We all wondered how much longer Betty would hang on.

"You've got to get some sleep," I told Cheryl gently. "I'll stay right here with her. I promise I won't leave her side."

She reluctantly went to the adjacent bedroom and lay down, and I took up the vigil next to Betty. Her breathing was labored.

I didn't want to see Betty suffer, so I started praying. Cheryl could hear my murmuring through the wall.

God, send your angels to take Betty home. Don't let her be in pain too long. She's your child, and she's ready.

Praying felt like making a phone call to someone I'd been out of touch with for a long time. While I talked to God about Betty, my heart started to change. My connection with God was instantly rekindled.

If a child leaves home and doesn't talk to his father for years, is he not still his father?

Like the few other times I had talked to God in earnest, God responded right away. My prayers for Betty were answered within an hour. You really can't outdo or underestimate God.

As for me, I realized I had been gone way too long. It was time for me to come home to God.

ﮊﮊﮊ

Years earlier, right after Janet left me, I'd found myself aimlessly driving around the countryside one afternoon.

I stopped my white Chevy pickup truck in a driveway, turned off the ignition and stared blankly out the windshield.

Rap-rap.

The tap on the window startled me out of my haze. Was that Janet's uncle?

I rolled down the window.

"I'm sorry," I told the man, who was indeed the uncle I had met once for only a few minutes. He had taken our prom pictures. "I don't even know why I'm here."

He seemed unfazed.

"That's okay, son. I do."

I stepped out of the truck, and Janet's uncle led me into the house. My shoulders sagged under the emotional weight I carried. We sat down at the kitchen table with his father. Janet must have told them about our broken engagement, but that's not what they wanted to talk about.

"Do you know Jesus?"

I broke down crying. I had heard about Jesus in church, but I didn't have any kind of connection with God.

"No," I finally choked out.

"Would you like to?"

I'd prayed before, but it always felt empty. This time, I was so hurt that I was willing to try just about anything. If Jesus was going to help me, absolutely I'd give it a go.

"Let's pray." Janet's uncle clapped his hand on my back, and I bowed my head and prayed with him for Jesus to take over my life. I told God I was sorry for the bad things I had done.

In an instant, the crushing pain dissolved. For the first time in my life, I felt God touch me. I could smile, laugh and feel life. I had walked into that house feeling sick, and I left with my back straight and my heart free.

As real as it all was, it was easy to forget. I never talked to anyone about it. I certainly hadn't tried to find other Christians, and I didn't read a Bible or pray a lot. About a year and a half later, the whole God thing seemed distant. My life had taken a long detour.

കൈകൈ

Cheryl, who didn't have a relationship with God, panicked when her mom died. She didn't have anything bigger to hope in, and she was scared about her own eternity. She worked as an apartment manager, and one of her tenants offered to ask her pastor if he would conduct Betty's funeral.

We felt comfortable at the church that hosted Betty's funeral, and we soon joined Wednesday night Bible studies there. The men and women met separately, and Cheryl and I would often compare notes afterward.

Cheryl thought she had started a relationship with God 25 years earlier in a Baptist church, but now she wasn't so sure.

"I've never felt the hand of God on me," Cheryl told me. "I never physically felt a change because of God."

"Have you ever asked him to change you?" I asked.

I wondered if Cheryl had ever really talked to God about having a relationship with him or had ever told God she was sorry for the wrong things she had done in her life.

"I don't think so — I can't really remember."

"Maybe you should ask now."

That made Cheryl think. She was up all night thinking about how badly she wanted to see her mom again. She wondered if she had said she wanted a relationship with God all those years ago but never meant it with her heart.

The next morning, she burst into my office with a cup

of coffee. "Honey, guess what?" She was crying before I could answer.

I jumped out of my chair to hug her. What could be wrong?

"I've just been saved," she sobbed, and now I saw these tears were from joy, not sadness. "The Lord is in me, and I feel that so strongly. I feel God touching me."

She had felt God's presence when she was getting ready for work that morning, and it was so powerful that she had fallen on her knees in our house and told God she wanted a relationship with him. She felt so instantly happy and peaceful that she cried all the way to my office. Soon after, we were married.

৵৵৵

We got the heartbreaking news that Jack, who was now living in Nevada with Ellen, was dying of liver disease. A decade of heavy drinking had caught up with him. We prayed in our driveway before we left, our hearts heavy on what we thought was a trip to say goodbye to our beloved friend and brother. Our trip, however, ended up being a rescue mission.

When Jack's doctor delivered the surprising news that he might recover if he stopped drinking, we decided he and Ellen should move into our empty spare room in Oregon. Their place in Nevada was too far from medical facilities, and we lived five minutes from a hospital. They agreed.

We loaded Jack, Ellen and their 10-year-old daughter into our car. Jack was optimistic that he would make it for six months and then be put on a transplant list, but within a week of living in Oregon he was back in the hospital, his organs shutting down. We settled him into our home and brought in Hospice care.

Cheryl and I were devastated. We loved Jack so much, and we were hopeful that if we could help Jack know God before he died, we could have peace about his impending death.

I was surprised when Jack agreed to let one of our friends and our pastor come over and pray for him. The room filled with more people than we expected: Cheryl's daughter, a few people from the apartment complex, Jack's wife and daughter and two other pastors.

We talked with Jack, who was frail and yellowed from his liver shutting down, for a few hours. We were shocked when Jack asked to pray for Jesus to become part of his life — in a room full of people.

We had expected to pray that night that God would heal Jack's body, not knowing that God would heal his heart. After years of drinking, cooking meth and wanting no part of God, Jack asked Jesus to be part of his life.

If I had any questions about Jack's sincerity, they were answered in the next two days before Jack died. I woke up early to read my Bible, and about 6 a.m. each morning Jack walked in and asked to borrow a Bible. I directed him to the book of John, which he read for half an hour before putting the Bible back on the shelf.

THE FLOOD

God was showing me that Jack had really changed, that his prayer for God to save his soul was real.

I have assurance that Jack is with God now.

☙☙☙

The changes in our lives have been contagious. Like I assured Cheryl as we stood on the edge of the floodwaters in California, most of our family followed us to Nevada and some on to Oregon. Ellen, who we had abhorred for years, now lives with us. Our hard hearts toward her have softened as we've gotten to know her, and now she and her daughter go to church with us.

The Sunday after Jack died, Cheryl wasn't emotionally ready to go to church. Out on my own, I headed to a church that was a block from our house. We'd driven by it a thousand times, sometimes on the start of our 20-minute drive to the other church.

When I walked in the door, everybody wanted to meet me, showing a genuine interest in who I was. The atmosphere at Relevant Life Church felt almost like a living room, where you could feel the love of the church family surrounding you.

That afternoon, the first thing I told Cheryl was she had to try this church.

"I have yet to walk in a church that makes me feel like this church," I told her. "It's just so amazing."

The church lived up to my first impressions. We feel God's presence when we walk into the building. When we sing during the worship time, we sense God surrounding us.

I've also been volunteering at a prison for about a year and a half, and I've seen what a huge difference it can make for inmates when you take time to visit them. Because of what I've gone through with addiction, I can connect with inmates who have similar struggles.

ঞৰঞৰঞৰ

We've learned to turn everything in our lives over to God, and we see him working in the world all of the time.

Recently a cousin asked me to speak to her son, who looks like he is heading toward alcohol and heroin addiction.

What am I supposed to say to him? I wondered. I hardly knew the kid.

"You'll think of something."

I decided if an opportunity presented itself, I would take it, and the next day at a funeral service, I saw Ben sitting in a corner by himself. This was my chance. I knelt down next to him.

"I know the road you're going down, and you don't want to go down it." I hoped the sincerity in my voice registered with him. "From one addict to another, when you're ready to get rid of that pain, God will take it from you."

We sat in silence for a moment, and then he shook my hand and thanked me. I wondered if I'd gotten through to him. A few days later, my smart phone buzzed. Ben had sent me a Facebook friend request, reaching out to me.

In that moment, I was caught up in a flood all over again. God was on the move in this kid's life. How could I want anything more than to be part of God's plan to turn somebody away from a dangerous road I've already been down? His strong currents of love are overwhelming. They swept me away. I can't imagine living my life any other way.

THE FACE IN THE MIRROR
The Story of Pearl
Written by Karen Koczwara

No one knows my secret.

I force a smile as I twirl across the dance floor, my shiny dress swirling around my ankles and my long red hair swishing at my side. My partner smiles back, his breath just inches from my face.

Little does everyone know we only met an hour before. I know his first name, I know he is wealthy and I know that at the end of the evening he'll pay me plenty of money for this little charade. But he doesn't know my real name, my favorite color or what I did yesterday.

We are two strangers, twirling round and round — our worlds colliding for only a night.

A night he might always remember, but a night I will try hard to forget.

❧ ❧ ❧

I was born on February 16, 1939 in Oklahoma. My twin brother and I had five other siblings, so our house was always bustling with noise and activity.

When I was just a toddler, my father suddenly passed away, leaving my mother to care for us all alone. Needing a husband to take charge of the house, she married a rancher when I was 5.

We all settled into a small house in the country; our tight quarters required that I share a room with my parents. When I entered elementary school, my stepfather grew abusive toward my twin brother and me. Often I came home to find him beating on my brother, his fist raised in anger as my brother cowered in the corner.

"Don't let me see you do that again, kid!" my stepfather hollered, shoving my brother against the wall.

As my brother slunk off down the hall, my stepfather turned his anger on me. "And you, stupid girl! You think you can just waltz in here after going out leaving the house a mess? What sort of idiot are you, anyway?"

Tears burned my eyes as I ran off to find my brother. I dreaded running into my stepfather around the house and hated sleeping in the same room with him. I waited for my mother to step up and defend me, but she never said a word. And that was just the problem. As a little girl, I longed for my mother to say she loved me, but she never once uttered the words. What if I really was as unlovable as my stepfather made me feel?

At night, I waited in bed, hoping my mother might come in with a goodnight hug. But instead, she merely popped her head through the door when the lights went out. "Goodnight, Pearl," she called out from the doorway.

Would it hurt you to hug me? Just once?

Sometimes in the evenings, a neighbor lady took me to church. I liked the stories my teacher told about God, but I didn't understand how they might help me in real life.

"Shh, when you go up front to the altar, make sure you

don't make any noise," my Sunday school teacher whispered as we filed up to the front of the church for communion.

I obeyed as I shuffled to the front. God must be awfully important if we had to be quiet for him all the time.

To avoid my stepfather's wrath, I often slept over at a friend's house. There, we told silly stories and giggled ourselves to sleep in the safety of her room. I was thankful to be far away from the monster who yelled at me day in and day out. I poured myself into school and sports as I got older and enjoyed both. While playing sports, people applauded me and made me feel like a star; while at home, I felt like a nobody.

We moved out west to California, where I completed the rest of my high school years. I was a good girl, never one to drink or get into trouble, but I always enjoyed a good time. One Tuesday afternoon, my girlfriend and I took a bus from the suburbs into town to go skating. As we whirled around the rink, a handsome guy caught my attention. I blushed as our eyes met, my cheeks turning the color of my bright red hair. He skated over to me, and we began chatting.

"My name's Pearl," I told him. "You come here often?"

"Not really. I'm in the service, and I actually just got back from Germany yesterday," he replied. "Still trying to adjust to normal life again."

"Yes, I can imagine." As we talked, we discovered we had much in common, including the same birthday. Within no time we began dating, fell in love and married.

I was just 17, but it was the 50s, and I knew many girls my age who married young. I gave birth to a little boy a year later, and for a while our life felt complete. But soon, as newlyweds often do, we began to fight.

"Did you spend your whole paycheck on that car?" I demanded one evening, storming out to the garage where my husband tinkered under the hood of his car. He loved the classics, and I didn't mind his hobby until it came to our dwindling bank account. "We've got a son to provide for now, remember?" I reminded him of our new responsibilities as he popped up and wiped the grease off his hands.

"I work two jobs, Pearl. I deserve to have a little fun on the side, okay? Don't worry, we're not going to run out of money." He disappeared under the hood again, and I gave a defeated sigh as I shuffled back inside.

But we eventually did run out of money, and I grew worried. To supplement our income, I got a job at a local carhop as a waitress. As men wandered in to eat, I often lingered at their tables and flirted. They flirted back, and I enjoyed the attention. *My husband's too busy working on that darn car to even notice what I look like anymore,* I lamented. *Maybe we don't have as much in common as I thought.*

Our fighting escalated at home, and finally, my husband declared he was moving back to Ohio without me. I agreed to the divorce, as my heart had given up a long time ago. I had no idea how I'd manage as a single mother, but I'd have to find a way to provide for my son.

THE FACE IN THE MIRROR

I struggled to make ends meet, working long hours as a waitress while paying rent on a tiny apartment in the city. One day, as my shift ended, a fireman pulled up at the restaurant. He inspected me from head to toe as he ordered his food, and I expected he was about to flirt with me as the other men did.

"I know a lot of men who would love a redhead like you," he drawled, biting into his burger.

"Oh yeah?" I tried to stay cool as I counted back his change. I wasn't sure I was ready to jump into a relationship with any man after my divorce.

"Yeah. Say, I see you working hard here. Can't pay much more than minimum wage, right? Plus some change in tips maybe? Am I right?"

What was this guy up to? "Yeah, it's not exactly top money," I mumbled. "Got a son to provide for all by myself, so it's tough sometimes."

He nodded thoughtfully. "How would you like to make lots and lots of money?"

I raised my brow. "How?"

"You ever considered being a call girl?"

A call girl? "What exactly do you mean?" I pressed.

"Let's put it this way. There are a lot of very wealthy men out there who would pay top dollar to spend an evening with a pretty lady like you. You give them your time, they give you the money. I can guarantee it's much, much more than you'll ever make here," he added with a convincing smile.

I took a deep breath. I'd heard of call girls before, and

they didn't exactly have the best reputation. As I wiped my greasy hands on my dirty apron, I envisioned myself trading in tiring hours on my feet for romantic evenings in the city. "So by 'spend the evening,' what exactly do you mean?"

He looked me up and down again seductively. "It means you give them whatever they want. Like I said, you won't find better money."

"So, like a prostitute," I blurted.

"If you want to call it that. I think call girl sounds much more elegant. Look, most of these guys are unhappily married. They just want a pretty girl they can take to a party and romance all night long. Redheads are in top demand. So, I've given my pitch. What do you say?"

I was a 21-year-old single mother. He was right; I would never make much here at the carhop. I could spend the rest of my life struggling to pay my bills and support my son, or I could take hold of this once-in-a-lifetime opportunity and seize it. "I'm in," I agreed.

I wrote my number down for the fireman, my hands shaking as I slipped it to him. He called me later that week to set up my first "appointment." I would be escorting a wealthy doctor to a party in San Francisco and spending the night with him. My life of adventure, fairytale romance and big money was about to begin.

Or so I thought.

಄಄಄಄

THE FACE IN THE MIRROR

The sun streamed through the window of the hotel room as I blinked my eyes open. Beside me slept a man twice my age, his gray hair poking out from beneath the tangled covers. I quietly slipped out of bed and shuffled over to the window. The city of San Francisco was just waking up, too; cars blared their horns as they sped down the road, and businessmen in dapper suits marched down the street carrying briefcases. *One of them could be my client tomorrow night,* I thought to myself as I closed the curtains.

I pulled my stockings on, one leg at a time, then wandered into the bathroom to wash my face. The girl staring back at me smiled, but I hardly recognized her. Since becoming a call girl months before, I'd traded my soul for nights on the town with lonely, wealthy doctors and pharmacists. As I slipped on my sparkling party dresses and stepped into their cars, I forced a smile on my perfectly painted red lips and made small talk through the evening. In the morning, I wiped off the last traces of makeup, got dressed, collected my money and went on with my day.

Where did Pearl go? I wondered as I stared in that mirror, smoothing my rumpled hair and splashing water on my freckled cheeks. She was still in there, of course, but she'd been buried deep, replaced by a girl who went through the motions to pay the bills and put food in her son's mouth. The fireman had been right — the money was good. But it was a high price to pay for the heart I'd buried in the process.

To numb the emptiness inside, I began going to bars, drinking and dancing with my girlfriends. Deep down I hated my new life, and I hated myself for the person I'd become. I'd slept with more men than I could count, but none of them even knew my first name. I thought of the first day I'd met my ex-husband, how our eyes had met in that skating rink and locked for what felt like an eternity. I'd thought it was love at first sight. But now, I wasn't so sure I'd ever loved anyone or been loved by anyone in my life. My mother had never expressed her affection, and the only words out of my stepfather's mouth had been abusive. If no one loved me, what was the point in living anymore?

One night, as I lay on the couch with an empty bottle of booze at my side, I contemplated ending my life. It all seemed so pointless. I could care less about the money; I'd have been just as happy working at the carhop if I had true love in my life. But it was too late to go back now. I'd gotten myself in too deep, and it seemed impossible to scrape my way out of the mess I'd made.

What's the easiest way to die? I mulled this over in my mind for a while, until at last I stood up and shuffled into my son's room to check on him. Just 6 years old, he lay sprawled in his bed, his thick hair spread across his pillow as he slept peacefully.

He'd brought me so much joy in his short life, filling my heart in ways I never knew possible. How could I even think of leaving him? He'd be all alone, without a father or a mother, without *anyone* to love him. My life felt meaningless, but I would make the choice to live for my son.

"I will live for you," I whispered to him as I planted a kiss on his little head.

One day, my sister called and invited me to church with her. I hesitated to say yes. I'd attended church off and on over the years, but I hadn't gone in some time. I'd made up my mind to hate people because I hated myself, and I was afraid to get close to them for fear they might find out the truth about my real life and shun me.

"I dunno," I mumbled. "I'm kind of busy tonight."

"Please, Pearl? I think you'll really enjoy it," my sister pleaded.

I'd noticed a change in my sister since she started attending church regularly the past few years. She explained she had invited God into her life and that he was the reason she was filled with joy. Still, I wasn't sure this was the answer to my problems, nor was I sure I wanted to be like all those crazy church fanatics who went around reading their Bibles all day.

"I'll go," I agreed with a sigh. "But only because I love you."

I liked the church well enough; the people were friendly, and the message was encouraging. The pastor spoke about a God who loved everyone so much that he'd sent his Son, Jesus, to die on a cross for the wrong things they'd done. With Jesus, he explained, we could experience true forgiveness. I'd heard the message before, but I'd never been sure it was for me. After all, I'd done terrible things; my life was nearly in ruins. Could God's love really extend to me, or was it only for good people like my sister?

"What did you think about the message?" my sister asked on the way home.

I nodded. "It was nice," I said coolly.

That night, I had a few drinks and settled into bed. The pastor's message replayed over and over in my head. I did want what my sister had; she was full of peace, always laughing, always positive even when life didn't go her way. Most of all, she showed me unconditional love, never judging me but always calling with a word of encouragement to brighten my day. One thing was certain: Jesus was real in her life.

As I sat there on my bed, alone, I decided to pray and invite Jesus into my life. "Jesus, please come into my heart. I know I have done many wrong things, but the pastor says that no matter what we've done in the past, it's never too late to find you. Please help me to live for you. Give me the love my sister has so I can give it to others."

I waited a moment, almost expecting the skies to part and God to boom down from heaven with a resounding response. But the room remained quiet, and I wondered if I'd said the prayer correctly.

"Let's try this again," I said aloud. I repeated the prayer, more emphatically this time, adding an "Amen" on the end. And then I waited. But again, nothing happened. I felt like the same old me.

"Hmph. This is silly," I muttered to myself, yanking

the covers over my head. "I don't think it worked after all."

I drifted off to sleep, and when I woke up the next morning, I stumbled into the bathroom to wash my face as usual. As I stared in the mirror, I nearly gasped at what I saw. The girl staring back was stunningly beautiful. My eyes were crystal blue, and my skin glowed; not one of my freckles seemed to show. "I am the most beautiful person in the world," I whispered in awe.

What had happened to me overnight? Had my prayer worked after all?

I raced to the phone to call my sister, but she didn't answer. Dying to talk to someone, I called the pastor's wife. As I described what I'd seen in the mirror, I could hardly contain my excitement. "I don't mean to sound vain, but when I looked in that mirror, I'd never seen anything so beautiful," I gushed.

She laughed. "Honey, that's not vain. That was the Holy Spirit in you."

"The Holy Spirit?" I asked.

"That's right. When you ask Jesus into your heart, he sends his Spirit to live inside of you. The Holy Spirit prompts your heart, convicting you when you are wrong and encouraging you to make good decisions that please God. I'm so excited for you! You are truly beautiful, inside and out."

At 24 years old, I finally understood the amazing, transforming message of God's love. I finally understood why my sister's face glowed and her heart surged with joy. She knew Jesus, and now, at last, I knew him, too. My life would never be the same, for there was no turning back to my old ways.

I could hardly wait to go to church the following Sunday. As the music began that morning, my hand went straight up in the air, and I began to praise God.

"We were praying for you," several ladies in the church told me after the service. "We're so glad you're here and so happy you've invited Jesus into your life."

"Thank you," I replied, smiling. *I belong right here. I've never felt more at home than I do in this moment.*

I gave up my life as a call girl, trading fancy nights on the town and wads of cash for a job servicing machines at a cannery where my brothers worked. I was happy to give up my former job; waking up next to strangers had proven empty, lonely and unfulfilling. I now had something better than all the money in the world could buy: I had a new relationship with Jesus. Life in the fast lane had stripped my soul, but I had been restored by the one who had healed my heart.

I began reading my Bible, eager to learn more about God. Psalm 103:12 became one of my favorite verses: "As far as the east is from the west, so far he has removed our transgressions from us." God not only forgave all the wrong things I'd done in my life, he forgot them as well. It was as if they'd never existed! If he could forgive me, I could forgive myself.

I didn't date at all during the next few years. I desired to meet someone and get married again someday, but I trusted that God would bring him into my life in his perfect timing. A nice guy named Jim worked at the cannery and often came down to chat with me when I serviced the machines. I was impressed with how polite he was, but I never flirted with him as I assumed he was married.

One day, I showed up for work alone.

"Where's your husband today?" Jim asked.

"Oh, I don't have a husband. You must mean my business partner," I replied quickly.

"Oh, I see." Jim smiled and returned to his work.

The next time I returned, Jim announced he was going deer hunting with some friends. "I really don't know how to cook venison if I do catch anything," he told me.

"Why don't you bring me a recipe from your wife, and I'll see what I can do with it?" I suggested.

"Oh, I'm not married," Jim replied.

I hoped he didn't notice my face color at his response. *This whole time, I thought you were married, and you thought I was married! I thought you were too good to be true!*

"Oh," I replied casually. "I guess I, uh, assumed you were."

Shortly after we cleared this all up, Jim invited me on a date. "Do you like pancakes?" he asked.

I smiled. "Yes."

"I know this great pancake house. I'd love to take you there."

Jim and I had a wonderful date, but I knew I needed to address something important before things went any further. I took a deep breath. "Jim, I think you are a really great guy, but I'm a Christian, and I love God. I'm looking for someone who shares my beliefs."

"Oh. Well, I certainly understand," Jim said, nodding politely.

When I went back to service the machines, Jim met me at the door. "I've been thinking, Pearl, and I was wondering if I could go to church with you."

"Of course!" I replied eagerly.

Jim attended church with me the following Sunday, and as the service closed, he prayed and invited Jesus into his life. I was thrilled at his decision; he had found the same hope and peace I'd found in my life. We could now move forward together in our relationship.

Jim asked me to marry him, and I happily accepted. He had a young daughter from a previous relationship, and I took on the responsibility of raising her. I had always wanted a daughter and was happy to be a part of her life. My son was now entering his teenage years and gaining more independence; at last I had a complete family again.

One day, I went to visit my mother. She was now in her 70s, and her heart had softened over the years. As I shared with her the things God had been showing me, she listened intently.

"You know, Pearl? When you first started going to church, I told your sister that you'd better not become one of those crazy spiritual fanatics. But I really see a change in your life, and I know I need that, too. I hope it's not too late to invite Jesus into my heart."

"It's never too late," I assured my mother. "It will be the best decision you ever make."

My mother invited Jesus into her life, and as she began attending church and reading her Bible, she declared, "Jesus was the best thing that ever happened to me!"

I thanked God for answering my prayers and prayed that one day, all of my siblings would have a relationship with Jesus as my mother, sister and I did.

The kids grew older, and Jim joined the Merchant Marines. We enjoyed traveling together for the next several years, venturing all the way from Canada to Mexico and many places in between. I developed a passion for the outdoors, and Jim and I spent a great deal of time backpacking and hiking around various mountains and lakes. Now that I knew God, the creator of everything, I had an even deeper appreciation for nature. Jim and I began talking about getting out of the busy city and buying property in Northern California.

"I've heard it's real nice up by Mount Shasta," Jim said one day. "We should go check the area out."

We drove up to explore the area and fell in love with a tiny town near the beautiful snowcapped Mount Shasta. Jim decided we could buy a large piece of property in the country, and he would keep working in the Bay area for the time being. The idea of owning a house in the country appealed to me; I'd have plenty of time to explore nature and spend time with God in a rural, serene setting.

One evening, while Jim was out of town, I came home from church and suddenly felt very afraid. I hated being in the dark house alone; the stillness of the night was eerie and frightening. I rushed from door to door, checking all the locks and peeking out the windows into the blackness outside. Shuddering, I retreated to my bedroom, where I pulled out my Bible and flipped to Ephesians 2:1-3, which described Satan as "the ruler of the kingdom of the air."

"What does this mean, God?" I cried out. How was this verse supposed to comfort me?

And then, clear as could be, I sensed God say to me, "I am the king."

Of course! Satan may be the *prince* of the world, always taunting us and trying to discourage us, but God was the *king*. His power was greater than anything or anyone. He was the one who would protect me in the night, who would replace my nagging fears with peace and rest.

On impulse, I threw open the front door and yelled out to the cows in the field, "I know the king!" I nearly laughed as I shut the door. I had spent too long living my life in fear. If my God was in control, I needn't be afraid. He would protect me no matter where I was or what circumstance I faced.

My sister, who had led me to Jesus, passed away when she was 65 years old. I grieved her terribly; her joy had truly been contagious. At her funeral, 13 people came forward to ask Jesus into their heart.

"I knew your sister, and there was something definitely different about her," one lady told me. "She was always smiling, and I could tell her joy came from within. She really loved Jesus, and I want that same love in my heart."

How many others did my sister share Jesus with? I wondered as I glanced around the crowd. *God, help me to be like her, to share your love with that same enthusiasm everywhere I go.*

Jim and I grew restless and talked about moving again. We had always loved the ocean and found the Oregon Coast especially desirable. We moved to a beautiful little fishing community surrounded by tall pine trees, sand dunes and harbor views. I loved our peaceful life there, loved waking up to the crisp ocean air and the morning fog that drifted over the mountains each day. We found a church where we could settle down and met plenty of new friends in no time.

My daughter-in-law called one day with devastating news. My son's recent surgery hadn't gone well, and he'd suffered severe complications that had left him possibly disabled for life. Overnight, our lives were changed forever.

"Oh, God, please heal my son!" I prayed fervently. I couldn't bear the thought of my only child suffering for the rest of his life.

As doctors scrambled for answers, the fear I'd tried to put behind me crept up again. What if my son was never healed? I went to bed that night, tossing and turning, wondering how we'd all make it through this difficult time.

That night, I had a powerfully vivid dream. In it, I was cleaning the basement of our three-story home when I suddenly heard voices. They began as a low whisper and then got louder and louder, frightening me to the bone. I frantically looked around for a place to hide. Unable to find anywhere safe, I ran outside with my cell phone and decided to call for help. But before I could dial, a voice boomed down from heaven loud and clear: "I have given you power, dominion and authority."

When I awoke, my heart was still racing. I knew God had clearly spoken to me in that dream. *Power, dominion and authority.* Now that I had his Spirit inside of me, I possessed all three of those things. Satan would try his best to make me fearful, but I could conquer that fear because I had power in Jesus Christ. As one of my favorite Bible verses, 2 Timothy 1:7, reads, "For the Spirit God gave us does not make us timid, but gives us power, love and self-discipline." All of the anxiety about my son's situation quickly faded away, and God replaced that fear with a peace in my heart.

Though I loved our little coastal town, Jim wasn't so sure about living there long-term. "I don't know if this is the place for us," he told me one day. "Maybe it's a little *too* small-town."

"That's just what I love about it," I replied with a laugh. "I go down to the store and know 10 people. After living in the Bay area, I like this small-town stuff."

"We're getting older, though. I think we should be closer to the big city, near the better hospitals, you know?" Jim was in his late 70s now, and though he was in decent health, he often worried about our future.

THE FACE IN THE MIRROR

We prayed about where we should spend our remaining retired years, but before we could make a decision, Jim suddenly passed away. I was devastated by his death. God had given me a wonderful life with this man, full of happy memories, many travels and shared laughs. What had begun as a polite friendship had resulted in a romance that spanned several decades. How would I live my life without him?

I tried to acclimate to life as a widow. I had plenty to keep me busy, but I missed Jim terribly. Though I loved my small town and hated to uproot, I desired to be closer to my ailing son and my precious grandchildren. I knew my daughter-in-law could use my help with the kids, and I began praying about moving to Salem to be near them.

"If this is where you want me to be, please make it clear, God, and I will go," I prayed.

In March 2009, I made the move to Salem to be near my family. I immediately knew I'd made the right move, but I also knew I needed a good church.

Church had been an integral part of my life since I invited Jesus into my heart. I visited two churches in the area, but they weren't quite the right fit. One day, I flipped open the phone book and happened upon one called Relevant Life Church.

"I'll give this a try next Sunday," I decided.

The following Sunday night, I made the 10-minute drive through the back roads to Relevant Life Church, where a handful of friendly people greeted me at the door. "So glad you're here," they said. "Welcome!"

By the end of the service, I knew I'd found a place to call home.

"Thank you, God. Once again, you've shown me that no matter where I go, I am never alone."

❧❧❧

"You know what, Pearl? I always feel so happy when you hug me," my teenage friend said as she wrapped her arms around my waist one Sunday morning.

Her youth leader walked over and smiled at me. "This here is the neatest lady in the church," he said, nodding at me. "We sure love you, Pearl. You are a real blessing to all of us."

"Aw, thank you. I love you guys, too." My heart warmed as I hugged my young friend back. As I walked into the church service, I waved to several friends before taking my seat.

Never in my life had I imagined I could be this happy. God had truly given me a merry heart, and as I'd prayed all those years ago, I'd been able to share that heart with others, just like my precious sister had. Three of my brothers had invited Jesus into their lives in their later years, and I praised God for the good work he continued to do in my family's life.

Later that afternoon, when I got home, I stopped to glance in the mirror. The face staring back wasn't the porcelain-skinned face of my youth, but she was lovelier than ever because of one thing: She had Jesus in her heart.

THE FACE IN THE MIRROR

The girl of my youth had longed for love, but the woman I'd become had found true love and been set free. That love shone from the inside out, and I *was* truly the most beautiful person I'd ever seen.

A DOSE OF GOOD MEDICINE
The Story of Marty
Written by Karen Koczwara

"He can't breathe! Call for help!" I cried as my son collapsed to the ground.

My wife raced for the phone as I knelt down and pulled my son into my arms. I knew these asthma attacks all too well. Usually, they passed quickly with the help of an inhaler, but this time, it failed to work.

I tried to keep calm, but my heart raced wildly as my son began to turn blue. Quickly, I grabbed his face and breathed into his lungs.

Please, breathe. Please, breathe. C'mon, David.

"Help's on the way. The neighbor's coming over, and I called for an ambulance." My wife knelt beside me, her face pale and fraught as she rocked back and forth. "He's blue, Marty! He's turning blue!" she cried.

Keep calm, I told myself. *Your family needs you more than ever right now.* But my hands trembled as I cupped my son's face.

With each desperate breath, I prayed life would return to his lungs.

Breathe, David. C'mon, fight, David!

And then, David exhaled deeply, as if everything inside him had given up on the fight. And my heart nearly stopped.

UNDEFEATED

No, God, don't let this be his last! Don't let this be his last!

ॐॐॐ

Most little boys long for adventure from the time they take their first steps. They toddle after their fathers into the backyard, tromp through the mud and learn early on that a good fort can be built from nearly anything outdoors. And as they get older, they seek out high mountains to climb and boast to their friends when they tear up their first car. But sometimes these adventures take them farther, to other parts of the world they never dreamed they'd explore. And then they're in for the ride of their life.

My adventure began in Fairbanks, Alaska, on July 22, 1947. My parents moved there from Southern California, purchased several sledding dogs and pursued homesteading. But when I was just a few months old, we returned to Southern California. From there, we moved to Grants Pass, Oregon, where I spent the remainder of my childhood years.

Grants Pass is a small town in Southern Oregon, nestled along the gurgling Rogue River. Its rural terrain provides ample opportunity for boating, fishing, swimming, hiking and every other possible outdoor activity one can dream up. But as a young boy, I loved hunting and fishing with my father, playing with my chemistry set and golfing with my father and grandfather on the weekends. I later played on the varsity golf team in high school and proved to be a strong competitor.

One day, when I was just a young boy, I found a stash of magazines near my father's bed. Curious, I picked them up and flipped through them. My face turned red as I saw pictures of naked women inside. *Playboy*, the cover read. Both curious and ashamed, I sifted through for a few more minutes before setting them down. Though I promised myself I'd never peek at them again, the images remained burned in my mind.

When I was 17, my girlfriend invited me to church with her. My maternal grandfather had been a missionary in India, and I had always been curious about his travels and stories. But I had rarely been to church before and didn't know much about God. I agreed to go with my girlfriend just to be polite.

"So what did you think?" she asked me after the service.

"It was okay," I replied. The pastor seemed nice, and the story he shared out of the Bible was interesting. But I didn't really have time for God or church these days. I had my future to think about. I was determined to be an engineer, and that would require an extreme amount of discipline and energy.

After high school graduation, I broke up with my girlfriend and moved away to study chemical engineering at Oregon State University. The program was intense but didn't seem to be right for me. I switched to pharmacy school in my sophomore year. I met a few kids who introduced me to a group called Campus Crusade. Like my high school girlfriend, they believed in God and wanted to share him with others.

"You should come to one of our meetings sometime," my new friend encouraged me.

"I'll check it out," I promised.

I began attending Campus Crusade meetings. The people were warm and welcoming, and I admired their enthusiasm for God. I understood the basics: God was love, and he wanted us to share that love with others. It seemed like a nice enough concept; I was all for being a good person.

I went around campus with my new friends, trying to talk about God with other folks and invite them to our meetings. Deep down, I didn't quite understand what I was saying or doing, but it felt nice to belong to something and get excited about it. However, as time went by, I became intrigued by another college scene: the frat party crowd.

"Hey, Marty, what's goin' on, man?" A guy waved a beer bottle at me as I stepped through the doors of the frat house one Friday night. Pretty girls sat curled up on the couches, drinking, laughing and flirting. Music blared in the background, and everyone seemed to be having a great time.

"Keg's out back, or there's beer in the kitchen. You know the drill," the guy called out, stumbling as he staggered over to one of the pretty girls on the couches.

I didn't know the drill, but I was about to find out. I

wandered out back, where it seemed half the college campus had congregated. Pushing my way through the crowd, I grabbed a red cup of beer and downed it. Those Campus Crusade folks were missing out. *This* was where the real fun was!

The summer after my sophomore year of college, I met a pretty girl, and we began dating seriously. One day, she approached me with some shocking news.

"I'm pregnant, Marty," she whispered.

"Wow." I took a deep breath. "Well, what are we gonna do? I mean, we're too young to have a kid. We need to get through pharmacy school. There's no way we can do this right now."

"What do you suggest we do?" she asked, sighing. "I'm scared, Marty. Real scared."

"You know what? I bet they have someone who could take care of it up in Seattle. They've got that kind of stuff up there." I tried to stay calm as I comforted my girlfriend. I loved her, but neither of us was ready to be parents and settle down. We'd just have to find a way to take care of this so we could move on with our lives.

My girlfriend and I drove to Seattle, where we met with an illegal abortionist. "I can't help you, but you may want to go buy some quinine pills. That should do the trick," he told us.

We found some quinine pills and went back to our hotel, where my girlfriend took a handful of them. Within a few minutes, she became extremely sick and began vomiting and staggering around the room.

"Are you okay?" I asked, my heart racing with concern. What had we done? Maybe this was a bad idea after all.

"The whole room is spinning. I'm so dizzy," my girlfriend moaned, running to the bathroom again.

I watched helplessly from the doorway, my own stomach churning at the scene. This was definitely a bad idea.

"I guess I'll try to use a coat hanger," she moaned a few minutes later.

"No," I said firmly. "You're sick, and I'm sick of this, too. Let's forget this and get you to bed." Her face was pale and sweaty as I helped her into the bed, and she looked like she might pass out at any second. *Please, let her be okay.*

My girlfriend fell asleep shortly after, and I watched her closely from the bedside in the dark hotel room. Suddenly, things didn't seem so complicated anymore. Yes, we were young, but we loved each other. Two people in love could make things work, right? If we did not lose this baby, I would ask my girlfriend to marry me, and we would raise it together.

"Marry you? Are you sure?" My girlfriend's eyes were full of life again as we drove home the next day. "I thought you said we were too young and all that."

"I love you, and you love me. I know we still have to finish school, but we'll find a way to make it work. This baby must be meant to be." I smiled over at her. "So is that a yes?"

"Yes," she replied with a giggle.

We were married shortly after, and in March 1968, my new wife delivered a beautiful, healthy baby girl, Angela. I was just 20 years old and my new wife just 17; we were nearly kids ourselves. But we were excited to be parents and determined to make the best of our new life together.

We worked our way through college, and I graduated with a B.S. in pharmacy in June 1970. I completed my pharmacy internship and applied for medical school, but things all came to a halt when I got a letter in the mail. I'd been drafted into the Army to serve in Vietnam.

"Vietnam? Marty, that's so far away! Look how far you've come in your schooling!" my wife cried when I told her the news.

"I know, but what can I do now? I don't have a choice in the matter," I said with a sigh.

Fifteen days before I was to enter the Army, I received an invitation to attend medical school at Oregon Health Sciences University. I reported the news to my draft board, and they deferred me from going overseas. I would not have to leave my family and my new career after all.

"This is amazing news. I can't believe it," I told my wife excitedly. "I don't even have the best grades. I don't know how this has happened, but I'm going to make sure to put my whole heart into medical school." Only later would I realize just who had orchestrated these events that would ultimately shape the rest of my life.

I took my studies seriously, and soon my mediocre grades became top scores. I received a Health Professions

Scholarship from the United States Army and decided to become a doctor in the Army when I graduated. With a part-time job, a full load of classes and a family at home, my days were full, but at night, I still made time to party with our friends, drink and smoke marijuana.

One night, after a few beers, I went home with another woman and slept with her. Not long after, my wife confessed she wanted to go see an old boyfriend, and I agreed to let her go. Perhaps if we both had a little fun on the side no one would get hurt, and neither of us would feel guilty. My wife returned home after her rendezvous with the old boyfriend and shared what they'd discussed. "I like him, but I told him I want to be with you, and he agreed that we needed to keep our marriage together," she said. "Maybe we'll stay together, Marty."

"You're right. No need to mess with things," I agreed.

I graduated from medical school magna cum laude in June 1975 and signed up for an internship and internal medicine residency program in Denver, Colorado. My wife became pregnant again, and on May 16, 1976, she gave birth to a little boy, Christopher. We were elated, but shortly after he arrived, the doctors reported frightening news.

"Your son has a platelet count of 5,000. This is most likely due to your wife's condition. There could be potential bleeding in his brain, so we need to treat him as soon as possible to get that platelet count up."

My wife suffered from a rare condition called idiopathic thrombolytic purpura and had had her spleen out years before. The ITP had transferred to the baby, and now his life was in jeopardy. "Is he going to be okay?" I whispered, a lump rising in my throat.

"We're trying to stay positive," the doctor assured us.

The doctors administered IVs to our newborn son for the next several days, but he developed a serious infection called osteomyelitis in his forearm from the needles. As little Christopher lay fighting for his life in the NICU, my wife and I clung to each other, praying he would be okay. I hadn't talked to God much growing up, but I figured it certainly couldn't hurt to throw up a few prayers during our desperate hour.

Christopher's platelet counts slowly rose, his infection waned and finally we were able to go home. My wife settled into life with two small children while I focused on my residency program. A friend of mine gave me a book by two psychologists that argued that by having an open marriage in which both partners dated other people on the side, couples could actually help their marriage thrive. The idea intrigued me. My wife and I had certainly married young; maybe it wouldn't hurt to explore other relationships while still trying to keep ours intact.

I suggested the idea to my wife. "What do you think?" I asked her. "There will be no judgment on either side. You do what you want, I do what I want, no questions asked. But we stay together."

My wife shrugged. "It's not a bad idea."

One night, I dressed in my best clothes and wandered into a disco in downtown Denver by myself. Loud disco music blared, strobe lights danced across the darkened room and crowds of people milled around the bar, laughing and drinking. I strode up to the bar, ordered a drink and scanned the crowd for pretty women. After a few more drinks, I gained enough courage to brave the dance floor alone.

"You by yourself?" a pretty girl asked, sidling up to me. The strobe light splashed across her face, illuminating her long lashes and red lips.

"Yup. You?"

"Yes." She smiled, and we danced for a while.

"What's a guy like you doing in a place like this alone?" she asked as we stepped away for another drink.

"I'm actually married," I confessed. "But my wife and I, we have this sort of agreement. We're free to, uh, see other people."

"Ooh, I like that," she said coyly, sipping her drink.

I went home with the girl that night, and the following night, my wife got dressed up and went out on the town for her turn. We continued this lifestyle for the next couple of years, and for a while, it seemed to work just fine. From the outside, we looked like an average happy couple with two children. If no one got hurt, what was the harm?

In July 1978, I got a fellowship in endocrinology in Tacoma, Washington, and we moved back to the Northwest. We bought a house, which seemed like the next logical step in our marriage. But our debt grew, and the financial stress made me depressed. My wife and I began to cheat on each other again, and I convinced myself I could fill the emptiness in my heart with other women and more alcohol.

"I think I need my own space," I told my wife at last. "This just isn't working for me." I got an apartment of my own and continued going out at night, getting drunk and meeting up with other women. I met a pretty girl several years younger than me, and we began dating. I enjoyed having an attractive woman on my arm and hoped her attention would jar me out of my slump.

But one day, my girlfriend decided our relationship wasn't for her anymore. "I like you, Marty, but I can't do this. You're married, you have two kids … I need a guy who can commit to me, not just someone to sleep with."

Her words stung. I didn't blame her for ending things; she deserved better. But I didn't want to be alone again. My marriage was on the verge of crumbling; it seemed the book I'd read hadn't been right after all.

One night, as I sat home alone, wallowing in self-pity, I happened across an old box of items. In it, I found a book called *The Gospel of John* that one of my college friends had given me. As I thumbed through, I became intrigued by the person of Jesus. I had studied many other religious figures over the years, but none of them seemed to measure up to Jesus. Jesus was a loving man who defied the rules of the pious leaders and hung out with the lowly prostitutes and detested tax collectors. Though he never did anything wrong, he gave his life for those very people when he died on the cross for the wrong they had done.

As John 3:16 reads: "For God so loved the world that he gave his one and only Son, that whoever believes in him shall not perish but have eternal life."

As I pored over the book, tears streamed down my face. Though I had heard this message before, it suddenly hit me that Jesus had died for *my* many wrongdoings, or sins, on that cross! He loved me so much that he had paid the price for me so I could spend eternity with him if I trusted him with my life. *This* was the good news my college friends had been talking about.

"God, if you're real, show me!" I cried out. I wanted to believe in all of this, but I still needed more proof. I needed God to be *real* in my life.

A few days later, I went out to a discotheque and met another pretty girl. This time, however, something seemed different about her. I soon discovered just what that was: She loved God. We began dating, and she shared about her relationship with God.

"Marty, God has a plan for your life, and he loves you very much," she said. "He wants to have a relationship with you."

"I believe that Jesus died for my sins, and I think all this is wonderful, but I'm just still not sure this is all for me," I confessed.

The more time I spent with her, the more attracted to her I became. I seriously considered divorcing my wife for good and marrying this woman. She was beautiful and kind, and I admired the way she loved God so strongly. I decided to take things to the next level and booked us a trip to Hawaii for a week. We had a wonderful time swimming in the warm waters and strolling on the beach as the sun went down.

"You're different than any other girl I've dated," I told my new girlfriend. "I'm still trying to figure out what it is that makes you tick."

"As I told you, it's God. He has given me a joy in my heart that I just can't explain. You can have that same joy, Marty, if you invite him into your life."

"When we get back, I'd like to go to church with you," I decided. I still had many questions about God, but attending church seemed like a step in the right direction.

When we got home, I bought a Living Bible Paraphrase edition of the Bible and began reading it. Unlike some of the other versions I'd read, it was easy to understand, and many of the concepts my girlfriend had discussed with me suddenly came to life. I began sitting and talking about the Bible on the weekends, trading my empty Saturday nights at the discotheque for a more meaningful time with her. Slowly, the pieces began to fit together, and the skepticism in my heart started to melt. I now believed that God was real and knew that Jesus died for my sins. I had seen other people living out their faith in a tangible way and could not deny the obvious joy in their lives. I believed that the Bible was true and knew that I needed a Savior to forgive the wrong I'd done in my life. I was finally ready to own it all for myself.

On September 30, 1979, I stood before Life Center Church in Tacoma, Washington, and publicly invited

Jesus into my heart to be my Savior. The minute I said the words, I felt like the heavy weight I'd been dragging around my entire life was suddenly lifted, and it seemed I was floating on air for the next several days. I had Jesus in my heart! *He* was the missing piece in my life, the only one who could fill the emptiness inside. No girl at a discotheque, no drink, no career and no amount of money could give me the freedom, joy and peace that came from knowing God. I had truly found the secret to a meaningful life.

One evening, the pastor's brother came to speak at our church. He shared his experiences as a missionary in Calcutta, India, as he worked with the poor near Mother Teresa. I was intrigued by his stories and felt God tugging at my heart as he spoke.

"I'd like to invite those of you who feel God may be asking you to one day be a missionary to come forward so we can pray with you," he said as he closed.

I stood to my feet, and they propelled me to the front of the room, where I clearly sensed God say two words to me: "Medical missions." Excitement mounted in me as I returned to my seat. I didn't know what this entailed just yet, but one day, I hoped to find out.

I signed up for a class at Life Center Church and met other people who had recently given their heart to Jesus as well.

I also dove into my Bible, starting with the four gospels at the beginning of the New Testament. The more I read about Jesus, the more I fell in love with him. He was the real deal, and 2,000 years after the Bible was written, he was still changing lives, including mine.

"Do you want to start a Bible study together?" my girlfriend asked.

"Yeah, that would be cool," I agreed.

We began a new Bible study, and a dozen of my girlfriend's friends attended; many of them were excited to grow closer to God. I attended Bible study at church on Tuesday nights and then shared what I'd learned with our group on Thursday nights. I loved soaking it all in and was excited at how my life had truly been transformed. But there was still a huge part of my life I had yet to deal with, and it was time to face that part head-on.

I worked part-time jobs in emergency rooms in Centralia and Chehalis, Washington. Between patients, I tried to catch a few winks of sleep, but I often woke up agitated and conflicted. I loved my girlfriend, but I was still married to my wife, who also continued to date other people. Should I break things off with my girlfriend and go back to my wife, whom I wasn't sure I loved anymore?

"God," I prayed, "I want to do your will. I know I can't be double-minded. Help me to do what pleases you and to make the right decision."

I asked a guy at church for direction. "Just keep reading your Bible," he encouraged me. "All the answers are in there."

The more I read my Bible, the more I became convinced that I needed to break things off with my girlfriend. I was heartbroken, but I also knew it was the right thing to do. I began praying about my marriage and asked God to help me forgive my wife for the things she'd done. After all, God had forgiven me for all the things I had done.

One evening, my wife announced she was going out on a date. "Can you watch the kids for me?" she asked.

I took a deep breath. "Sure." Deep down, I wondered how we could ever reconcile things if she continued to do as she pleased. But I put on a smile as she dabbed on her lipstick and headed out the door.

After I put the kids to bed, I retreated to the living room and read a booklet about being filled with the Holy Spirit. I started to pray. Suddenly, I began speaking in a special language and felt an indescribable peace in my heart. When I opened my eyes, I knew what had happened. I had been filled with the Holy Spirit, as our pastor often talked about in church. I knew now, more than ever, that God was real and that he would work all things in my life for his good.

"Are you willing to go to counseling?" I asked my wife when she got home.

She agreed, and we attended counseling the following week. But after just one session, she decided she was done. "I can see you're not the same person you used to be," she said. "I'm happy for you, Marty, with your new church life and all, but I just don't want to go that same direction right now. I'm sorry."

"I understand," I said sadly. "I hope that one day you find the same peace and joy I've found with God."

A DOSE OF GOOD MEDICINE

One day, my wife announced she was moving to Spokane with her new boyfriend and the children. I was devastated by her decision, but instead of letting my anger get the best of me as it normally did, I asked God to help me show her love. Just before they left, she asked me to come over and talk to her and her boyfriend about God. I obliged, and they listened politely as I shared about my newfound faith.

"Well, that's great for you, Marty. Not sure it's for us right now, but thanks for sharing," her boyfriend said coolly. "You take care of yourself now."

Well, God, I tried to share your love with them. I pray one day they will both come to know you.

Over the next several months, God did a transforming work in my life. He revealed many areas in my life I needed to address, including my foul mouth, my anger problem and my partying lifestyle. One evening, I attended a Christmas party and had a cocktail for the first time in months. As the night went on, I became so drunk I could not drive home. The incident shook me up, and I decided I'd never touch alcohol again.

A nurse at the hospital where I worked particularly got under my skin. Often, I escaped to the exam room, where I stuffed my head under a pillow, turned beet red and let out a deafening scream. As the weeks went by, I learned to take this anger to God instead of taking things out on my co-worker, and soon, I was able to see her through God's eyes. I asked for help with my foul mouth, and God replaced the swear words with words of praise for him.

My wife officially filed for divorce. Because Washington was a no-fault divorce state, I was forced to pay for the divorce. I sent her flowers and made one last attempt to reconcile, but she made it clear she was done. My heart was sad. Though we had spent many years being unfaithful to one another, we shared two beautiful children and had made many memories. But I'd done all I could do, and it was time to leave my circumstances in God's hands and trust that he had a good plan for my life, just as my old girlfriend had once reminded me.

In June 1980, the Army moved me to San Francisco, where I worked as Assistant Chief of Endocrinology for the first year and then was promoted to Chief of the Endocrinology Department for the next two years at Letterman Hospital, an Army teaching hospital. I welcomed the change of scenery and a chance at a new life. I loved Washington, but it was time to put my painful past behind me and look forward to the future.

I joined the Full Gospel Businessmen's Fellowship and became secretary and later president of the Petaluma chapter. I became involved in nursing home visits, a medical missions trip to Guadalajara and feeding the poor at a soup kitchen each Sunday. When a friend told me about a ministry to prisoners at San Quentin, I was eager to join. San Quentin is one of the roughest prisons in the country, which includes California's only gas chamber and death row and has housed some of the most notorious criminals in history. What better place to show God's love and share my story with those who needed a powerful message of hope? I seemed to be in training for something more.

Since inviting God into my life, I saw my medical career not just as a job, but as a way to reach out to others. I often prayed with my patients. Once, a lady came to me, especially distraught. "I have malignant melanoma, and I've been told there's nothing more that can be done," she said with a heaviness in her voice.

"May I pray with you?" I asked.

She agreed, and I prayed, asking God to heal her. A few months later, she reported wonderful news; she was cancer free! We praised God together, and once again, I was reminded of the power of prayer.

During my time in San Francisco, I found a wonderful church, Adobe Christian Center, in nearby Petaluma. I loved the warm atmosphere and great teaching and soon looked for ways to get involved. Before long, I found my place in the church choir and volunteered to teach Sunday school. My life was starkly different than what it had been just a few short years before, when discotheques were the highlight of my weekend and Sunday mornings meant hangovers and remorse. I thanked God daily for the work he had done in my heart and for the things he continued to teach me as I studied the Bible and attended church.

In October 1983, I completed active duty with the U.S. Army and began to pray about the next chapter of my life. My ex-wife had remarried, and both my children still lived in Spokane. I longed to be closer to my kids and decided to pursue jobs in Washington and Oregon. I interviewed for a job in my hometown of Grants Pass, but ultimately I settled in Salem, Oregon, and started a private endocrinology practice with Dr. Charles Campbell. I was praying for a lady going in for back surgery when God spoke to my heart. "I love Dr. Campbell, and I love Dr. Campbell's patients." I knew that Dr. Campbell's practice was God's choice for me.

Dr. Campbell and I quickly became good friends, and I enjoyed his company when the weekends grew long and lonely. Just before Christmas, Dr. Campbell came to me with a gleam in his eye. "All right, Marty. I know this is a bit out of left field, but would you consider going on a blind date? My wife and I know this really great lady."

I smiled. "Maybe," I replied with a shrug. "I guess it would be good to get out there again."

"She's real pretty. Petite, fair-skinned, brunette. I think you'll really hit it off with her."

"I'm game if she is," I said with a laugh.

Right after Christmas, I met Rhonna for our blind date. She was indeed very pretty, and I liked her sweet spirit right away. We began dating and fell in love. On April 29, 1984, I asked her to marry me. We wed in a beautiful ceremony at Calvary Temple Assembly of God Church in Salem, where we both attended, on August 17 that year. Just a few months after our wedding, Rhonna had some news for me.

"I'm pregnant," she announced. "Looks like you're about to become a dad again!"

I was thrilled. I loved my two older children and had

always wanted a larger family. "That's wonderful news!" I cried. *Thank you, God, for restoring my life and blessing me above and beyond what I could ever have imagined. You have truly brought my life full circle.*

Rhonna gave birth to a little boy, Isaac, in September 1985. I was excited to be a father again and loved watching Rhonna with our newborn son. "You're a natural," I told her. "I think you could have a dozen more."

In March 1988, Rhonna gave birth to another son, David. While our family was growing, something else inside of me was, too: a desire for medical missions. I remembered God's words for me back in Tacoma; I had clearly sensed him leading me in this direction. I spoke with Rhonna about it, and she agreed I should go.

"God has given you a gift, Marty, and I know you will use it to touch and heal many people, not just physically, but from the inside, too," she encouraged me.

I took several medical mission trips during the next few years, traveling to Guatemala, Belize and Mexico. I enjoyed them thoroughly and was able to serve the native people there and offer many practical skills. But something else stirred inside my heart, and I sensed God was about to do something even bigger.

In May 1992, I visited Tulsa, Oklahoma, where I learned about a ministry using professional people to reach the unreached people groups. One night during a teaching session about Muslims by an Iranian evangelist named Reza Safa, I sensed God clearly telling me that I was to prepare to go to a predominantly Muslim country in the near future. I ran to the front of the room for prayer.

When Reza prayed for me for boldness to reach Muslims, I got down on my knees at the back of the room and cried out to God. He started to show me a specific timetable to get out of my practice in Salem and be ready to go fulltime.

God, if that is what you are calling me to, I will be ready to do your work.

I went home and talked with Rhonna about the idea of permanently moving overseas. "What do you think? I know it would require big change, but I clearly believe this is what we're to do."

Rhonna was quiet a moment and then broke into a smile. "I'm on board, Marty. It will be an adventure."

We continued to pray and put together a timeline of when I would leave my practice and go into mission work overseas fulltime. But in October 1992, our plan was threatened when I received the phone call that is every parent's worst nightmare.

"Marty?" It was my ex-wife on the other line, and she was hysterical. "Angela's been in a really bad car accident. You'd better get up here as fast as you can."

"Car accident?!" My hands shook as I tried to hold on to the phone. "Is she okay? What are the doctors saying?" I cried.

"She's in a coma at Harborview Hospital in Seattle. Just come as soon as you can."

I hung up and sank to my knees. *God, please, let*

Angela be okay. Please, don't let her die! Don't let my baby girl die!

I made the long drive north, crying out to God the entire way. *Please, God! Please heal my daughter!* As I poured my heart out to him, I was reminded of an incident years before when Angela had nearly drowned at a pool party. God had spared her life then and answered our prayers, and he could do it again. Suddenly, an indescribable peace overcame me as I placed my daughter in God's hands, right where she belonged. I was a doctor, but *he* was the great healer.

When I finally arrived at the hospital, I raced into ICU, where my ex-wife met me at the door. Her face was pale as she explained what had happened. "Some drunk driver from Alaska came down to Seattle, probably to blow all his fishing money in the city. He plowed right into Angela's friend's car, where she was the passenger. His truck landed on the windshield and came down on her head. She has what the doctors call hemorrhagic contusions of the frontal lobe of the brain. She's in a coma, and that's all we know for now. Oh, Marty, I'm scared …" Her voice trailed off as tears spilled down her cheeks.

"Let's pray right now," I suggested, trying to keep my voice steady. I bowed my head and asked God to touch and heal our precious daughter. As the machines whirred around us and doctors barked out orders, I tuned it all out and focused on one thing: God's promises. I had relied on them before, and I would rely on them again. I had no choice but to trust in him.

The next morning, to our astonishment as well as the doctor's, Angela awoke from her coma. "This is amazing," a doctor proclaimed. "We've been monitoring her skull pressure, and it seems she's almost back to normal. It's really miraculous."

As my daughter's eyes fluttered open, my face broke into an irrepressible smile.

Thank you, God. It truly is miraculous. You healed my daughter!

Just a few short weeks later, Angela returned to her job as an assistant manager at a retail clothing store doing all of her previous duties. I continued to praise God for our miracle. Angela could have easily been killed, but God had spared her life. The incident could have discouraged us as we prepared to go overseas, but instead, we only grew more excited about our adventure. Much was still unknown, but I was confident God would take care of the details.

In November 1992, Rhonna and I took a trip to Almaty, Kazakhstan, with a group of medical missionaries from Tulsa, Oklahoma. A Soviet city, it boasted drab concrete buildings, crowded streets named after Soviet heroes and stores with sparse selection. There was much poverty and not just physically, but emotionally and spiritually as well.

During the first week of our visit, we held an outreach for many professionals in the city and attracted more than 700 people. We offered free medical care and medication to more than 900 patients and were able to tour the medical facilities in the city. We fell in love with the people and prayed about returning fulltime.

Our second week there, we held Bible studies and explained the basics of Christianity to many of the locals. At the end of the conference, more than 150 people came forward for prayer and healing and to invite Jesus into their heart. As I watched them weep on their knees and thank God for their healing, my heart surged with joy.

This is where you will return, I sensed God say to us as my wife and I prayed about coming back.

Before we left, the chief doctor of the city pulled us aside. "We'd like you to come back as a fulltime endocrinologist," she said.

"We will be back," I promised.

In July 1993, I left my practice, and our family made the big move overseas to live in Almaty fulltime. Pastor Kim, a Korean missionary pastor, connected us with women who helped us find food and translated for us. We were touched by their hospitality and thanked God for sending them to meet us.

Rhonna gave birth to a little girl, Aliia, in our apartment that September. A son, Sam, followed not long after. Our family was now complete, but our mission to Central Asia was just beginning. Before we left Oregon, we had started a non-profit organization that involved shipping hospital beds, drugs and other medical supplies from the Pacific Northwest. In 1995, we started a Christian clinic in Almaty and a smaller clinic in nearby Village-Tagar in 1998. We were able to see patients for a very reasonable fee and give out medications for free. We also secured portable dental chairs and did in-home medical visits for those who could not get to the clinic.

"I can't believe all God is doing here," I marveled to Rhonna. "This is far more than I ever could have imagined." It humbled me to think that the little boy from Grants Pass, Oregon, who spent his days tinkering with a chemistry set, would one day have the opportunity to reach thousands of Central Asian people not just with medical care, but with the good news of Jesus as well.

In addition to medical challenges, I saw another rising problem in the city. The illegal narcotics industry had grown, and children as young as 10 years old had become drug addicts. With the help of Pastor Kim and Doug Boyle, a missionary from Australia, we began Teen Challenge Kazakhstan at Grace Church in Almaty. This would one day become the largest Teen Challenge program outside the United States. Once again, I was humbled by the work God accomplished as we stepped into unfamiliar territory to serve him. I had no idea how long we'd stay overseas, but I planned to be there as long as God used me.

In 2001, our son David had a terrible asthma attack and became extremely agitated after his inhaler failed to work. After collapsing, I frantically attempted CPR while my wife called for help. David became blue, and I panicked when he exhaled what I believed to be his last breath. At that very moment, the paramedics arrived, and David vomited. A second ambulance arrived, and the paramedics administered a breathing tube to get his oxygen going and transported him to the nearest ICU.

"I thought we lost him," I sobbed into Rhonna's arms after they arrived. "But he's going to be okay. God brought them just in time." Even halfway across the world, God was still watching over us.

In 2002, God moved our family back to the United States. Our time in Kazakhstan had been unforgettable, but it was time to return to the place we called home. I started a solo practice, Willamette Valley Endocrinology, and now have three physician's assistants. I prayed my office would be a place of hope and healing for each person who walked through the doors.

Over the next several years, I began to pray about one more area in my life I still struggled with. Since my childhood when I'd seen my father's *Playboy* magazines, I'd fallen into pornography. Though I'd cut off my adulterous lifestyle years before, the pornography had remained a temptation, like a cookie jar I sneaked into every now and then when I needed a quick sugar fix. I prayed and asked God to take all my lustful desires away and asked several friends to pray for me and hold me accountable. Eventually, I found freedom from this struggle and thanked God for helping me to overcome it. Just as my favorite Bible verse, Philippians 4:13, promised, "I can do all this through him who gives me strength." It was God who gave me victory.

Our family returned to Relevant Life Church, formerly Calvary Temple Assembly of God Church. I became an elder and church secretary and enjoyed the wonderful friendships, teaching and worship we found there. Relevant Life had played a significant part in my spiritual journey before going overseas, and I was happy to call it home once again. My son Chris, who had struggled with his own addictions for years, gave his life over to God and became a pastor in Sandpoint, Idaho. I praised God for the work he had done in all of our lives.

❧❧❧

"Don't give Grandpa a scare like that again, okay?" I planted a kiss on my sweet little granddaughter's cheek.

Four-year-old Mollia looked up at me with her big brown eyes and nodded. "Okay, Grandpa," she said in a small voice.

Our family had decided to take a cruise to the Mexican Riviera in March 2011. We all looked forward to a week of relaxation, warm weather and family bonding. My son Isaac brought along his adorable daughter, Mollia, and we were all enjoying a day at the pool when Mollia slipped in and silently sank to the bottom. She was blue when Isaac pulled her out and began to quickly administer CPR. After what felt like hours, she finally vomited and began to breathe normally. We all praised God for averting our family from what could have been a horrid tragedy.

As I sat with Mollia at the ship's medical center where she recovered, I thought back to Angela's near drowning as a child, to her car accident and to David's near-death asthma attack. There had been so many moments that could have been their last, but God had spared them all. In the same way, he had spared my life, not just from earthly disaster, but from eternal death as well. I had once been a wayward, destructive young man, but through God's grace, he had blessed me with a wonderful life I never had imagined possible. Despite my hurts and failures, he had picked me up and planted me back on my feet, allowing me to use my medical knowledge to heal others and share his good news around the world.

God was the best doctor around; he had healed my heart. And his antidote was unconditional love, the best medicine of all.

LIKE A ROCK
The Story of Annie
Written by Karen Koczwara

My first DUI. I can't believe it.

I stare out the window of the cop car as the icy roads whiz by.

How could I have been so dumb? I should have known better than to down those beers before driving myself to rehab. I'm a real mess.

My pulse quickens as the police station comes into view. I've never been booked for anything before. I've been driving drunk for years, but this is the first time I've been caught.

I'll have to tell Dave. He'll be so angry. He's already fed up with me. But then, can I blame him? Look who I've become. My relationship with my sons is strained, and my daughter is following in my footsteps, her marriage in shambles. I can't stay sober for more than a few hours; my life is a continual disaster.

As the police officer escorts me inside the station, I stare at the ground, ashamed. In the past, if things got tough, I just ran. But I can't run right now, and I can't hide from my problems anymore. I'm at my end, and I need help. Now.

❧❧❧❧

UNDEFEATED

I was born on April 24, 1954 in Loveland, Colorado. A year later, my parents moved my older brother and sister and me back to Lexington, Nebraska, where they were originally from. Just a year later, they moved again to Nampa, Idaho, hoping perhaps the grass was greener over there. But this was where my nightmare began.

When I was 3 years old, my brother, six years my senior, babysat me one afternoon when my parents were gone. He wandered into my room as I played and sat next to me on the bed. I remained still as he touched me inappropriately and then slipped out of the room. I wasn't sure what had just happened, but I was definitely certain I didn't like it one bit.

One day as I played in my room, two teenage neighbor boys sauntered in, followed by my brother. "Whatcha doin', sissy?" my brother asked, sidling up to me.

I set down my dolls. "Nothing," I said in a small voice.

The boys stooped down and touched me as my brother had. I winced, closing my eyes so I couldn't see theirs. When at last they left, I went back to playing dolls, returning to a make-believe place where boys didn't do ugly things.

As a child, I adored my father more than anything. He taught us how to fish and play baseball and even planted cherry tomatoes in the garden so we could snatch them off the vine and eat them anytime we liked. I loved to put on my pajamas after dinner and run to climb in his lap. But one evening, as I eagerly jumped into his lap, he pushed me away.

"We don't do that anymore," my father said gruffly. "Run along now."

I ran back to my room and burst into tears. Why wouldn't Daddy let me sit in his lap? I thought I was his little princess. My mother didn't hug me much anymore, either. Had I done something wrong?

In 1961, we moved back to Loveland, Colorado, to be near our cousins. They had a wonderful tree house I longed to explore, but they had certain rules for those who visited it.

"You want up in that tree house? Then you gotta come with us," said my cousin, five years older than me, motioning toward the large empty field out back.

"Okay," I agreed, scampering after my cousins and brother into the field. Perhaps they wanted to play some sort of game. I liked games; this could be fun.

"Now pull down your pants," my cousin instructed when we'd waded deep into the field.

I bit my bottom lip and dug my feet into the dirt. "What for?" I demanded. I didn't like this game already.

"You want in the tree house? You gotta go by our rules." My cousin glared at me.

I didn't want to be left out of their fun, and I certainly didn't want to miss a chance to climb up in that tree house. I obeyed, and a few minutes later, we all ran back to the tree house as though nothing had happened. As I climbed the wooden rungs high into the tree, excitement mounted in me. I was finally one of the big kids now! The moment I reached the top, I took a deep breath and looked down from above. But as my eyes fell onto the field, I suddenly felt sick.

My mother found out what the boys had done to me in the field. But instead of turning her anger on them, she lunged at me, grabbed me by the collar and beat me until my head spun and my little body ached. "I don't ever want to hear about that sort of stuff going on again! You hear me, young lady?" she screamed.

I dabbed at my bleeding lip and nodded as tears filled my eyes. "Yes, ma'am," I mumbled, trying not to cry. After she stormed out of the room, I let the tears flow, salty as they stung my cheeks and ran over my mouth. I hadn't done anything wrong. Why was *I* the one to get in trouble? It wasn't fair!

My brother never touched me again, but the damage to my heart was already done. We moved back to Nampa, Idaho, the following year, and I started yet another new school for third grade.

By now, I'd learned two social tricks. I either withdrew and became a loner, or I transformed into the most outgoing, popular girl in the class. The nice thing about moving so much was that I could scope out the situation and decide who I wanted to be, much like an actor in a play. If things didn't work out, I took assurance in knowing we'd move again soon.

Sure enough, a year later, my mother announced we were moving to Boise. There, she gave birth to another little boy. After nine years, I was no longer the baby in the family. I hated my older brother for what he'd done to me, but I figured a newborn in diapers couldn't do much harm.

One afternoon, I noticed the next-door neighbor out on her porch, sipping a beer as she relaxed. *That looks pretty good,* I thought to myself. *And she looks cool drinking it. I wonder what beer tastes like.*

"Can I have a sip of your beer?" I asked my father a few nights later as he popped open a can after dinner.

"I guess so."

As the cool drink trickled down my throat, I let out a loud "ahhh" as I'd heard the neighbor lady do. "That's good!" I exclaimed. "Can I have more?"

"No, kiddo. Not now."

I made up my mind right then and there that I liked beer. I would find another way to get a hold of it someday soon.

At the beginning of sixth grade, we moved back to Nampa, Idaho. After just a few months, we moved to another small town, Hailey, and then back to Boise that same year.

My father was in the sheet metal industry and was always able to find work, but I was tired of moving and didn't understand why we had to do it so much.

"This is my third school this year," I complained to my mother as I got dressed one morning. "Why do we move so much? Why can't we just stay in one place like everyone else?"

"It's an adventure, don't you think?" my mother said. "New people to meet, new places to explore. I just hate stayin' in one place too long, wondering if there's something better out there."

"Well, I don't like it," I retorted. I'd given up on making good friends. What was the point when I'd never see them again in a few months?

In 1967, we moved to Tacoma, Washington, where I started junior high. My mom took us to a local church, and I enjoyed learning about God. My Sunday school teacher spoke about him as someone we could rely on no matter what, someone who remained the same when everything else seemed to change or fall apart. I thought of my brother's horrible acts, of my parents' lack of affection for me and of our many moves over the years. I'd never been able to depend on anything or anyone. Could God really be different?

As I continued to attend church, my heart warmed to the idea of God. My Sunday school teacher explained that we could have a relationship with him if we invited him into our life, and I wanted to do just that.

One Sunday, I went forward after the service and asked him into my heart. But as I walked back to my seat, I wondered if it had worked. *Maybe I didn't say the prayer right,* I thought to myself. *Maybe I should say it again. What if God didn't hear me or didn't like what I said?*

I went forward several times to ask God into my heart, but I still wasn't sure I'd done it right. At last, I decided maybe I just wasn't meant to be one of God's kids after all. I didn't know if my own parents loved me; how could God really love a naughty girl like me?

LIKE A ROCK

When I was 15, my sister was date raped and became pregnant. I heard my parents talking in hushed tones down the hall at night as they discussed her predicament.

"Are you scared?" I asked my sister.

"A little," she confessed. "I heard Mom say something about a home for unwed mothers. I might have to go away for a while."

I gasped. "Go away? Why can't you just keep the baby?"

She shook her head and sighed. "I don't think that's an option. They don't want me to be an embarrassment around town."

"But it wasn't your fault!" I cried.

My parents sent my sister away to a home for unwed mothers, and after she gave birth, she gave the baby up for adoption. I was devastated. How could they have made this decision for her? When my sister came back a few months later, her stomach was flat again, and so was her smile.

"No going out late for you, young lady," my mother said one night as I headed out to a friend's house. "You better be back by 9:00 sharp."

"Nine? That's so early!" I protested. Since when had my parents become so strict?

"No arguing. I can't have you off getting into trouble like your sister did," my mother replied. "I thought she was the tame one, but look what happened to her."

On New Year's Eve, I babysat for a lady down the street. After she and her husband left, I found their liquor cabinet and opened a few bottles. I got drunk for the first time in my life and passed out on the couch. When the woman came home, she had trouble waking me up.

"I must have, uh, dozed off," I mumbled sheepishly.

I started high school and began dating a guy named Pete. Not long into our relationship, he insisted I sleep with him. "If you love me, you'll go all the way," he pressed.

I relented and lost my virginity to him. I hated the entire experience, but I was desperate to be loved and was afraid I'd lose Pete if I didn't do as he said. I began sleeping with him regularly and partying with him on the weekends. We knew several older kids who knew how to get their hands on alcohol. Before long, I started drinking, too. This time, instead of just a sip, I downed one beer after another.

"You ever tried weed before?" Pete asked me.

"No."

"C'mon. You should try it. It'll relax you," he insisted.

"I'm good," I said nervously. I knew lots of kids who smoked pot, but I was afraid I'd choke on the smoke and look stupid. Instead, a short time later, I tried mescaline, a hallucinogenic, with a friend. I liked the way it removed me from reality. These days, my reality wasn't too great.

One evening, after I returned home from spending time with Pete, I found a note. It was written in my mother's fiery red lipstick and read, "No wonder you don't have any friends anymore. You smelled like a whore when you left the house tonight."

Her words seared my heart. I knew I was far from perfect, but how could my own mother say such a thing? Didn't she love me at all?

I started a new high school the following year but continued to date Pete. He was rude, mean and pushy; we broke up often but then got back together. During one of our breakups, I discovered I was pregnant. I panicked; what if my parents found out and sent me away like they had my sister? I could never give the baby up for adoption.

"I'm pregnant," I told Pete over the phone. "Just thought you should know."

"I'll pay for an abortion," he said quickly. "You can't have that baby."

"I've thought about keeping it," I said quietly.

"You can't, Annie. Are you crazy? You don't even have your driver's license yet!"

"You're right, I guess. I'm too young," I replied, sighing sadly.

Pete drove me to an abortion clinic, where I went through with the procedure. I was quiet as he drove me home that afternoon.

"So, no big deal, right?" he said coolly.

"No big deal," I replied numbly. I didn't like what I'd done, but what choice did I have? Pete wouldn't support a baby, and my parents certainly wouldn't. I couldn't risk losing what little I had. I'd just have to put the whole experience behind me and move on.

But a week later, while working at my new job at Sears downtown, my stomach began to cramp terribly. I raced into the bathroom, where my head grew light as the pain increased. When I stumbled out, pale and sweaty, my co-worker approached me.

"You don't look well," she said with concern.

"I'm not. I think … I think I need to go to the hospital," I stammered.

I checked into the emergency room and soon learned I had suffered complications from the abortion. The physical pain was excruciating, but the emotional pain was worse.

I was overcome with guilt, knowing my parents would be furious when they discovered what I'd done. *I'm proving my mom right, becoming the whore she says I am.* When my parents arrived, I had no choice but to tell them what I'd done.

"An abortion? Really, Annie?" my mother said in disgust. "How could you be so stupid?"

"That boy only wants you because you'll sleep with him," my father added, glaring at me.

When I got out of the hospital, I continued drinking and began smoking pot and taking LSD. I no longer cared about anything; I was numb to the world. I got a new job at K-Mart and found a used car for $50; I saved up two weeks' paychecks to pay for it. My mother had promised I could drive if I paid for my own insurance.

"What about that money I gave you for insurance?" I asked her.

"I had to spend it on that hospital bill of yours," she replied, glaring at me. "It's all gone."

"How could you? That was my money!" I stormed out of the room, slamming the door behind me. I wasn't proud of my abortion, but I certainly hadn't expected my parents to react so angrily. I graduated high school early and moved out of my house and in with a friend. I didn't speak to my parents for the next several months.

I took driver's education so I could get my license as soon as possible. One day, I drank several beers before hopping behind the wheel of the driver's ed car. To my surprise, I maneuvered the car well, stopping at all the lights and keeping to the speed limit.

"I'm really impressed. You're a great driver," the teacher told me.

Yeah, a great drunk driver, I thought to myself with a chuckle.

One day, my mother called. "Just wanted to let you know we're moving back to Nebraska," she said. "I don't expect you to go with us, of course."

"Fine. I don't plan on it," I replied coolly. Deep down, I was homesick and missed my parents, but I wasn't about to tell my mother that. However, a few months later, I gave up my pride and moved back to Nebraska to be with them. My father was still very angry with me, and we avoided each other's eyes as we passed in the hallway.

That fall, I met a guy named Randy. We began dating and spent our evenings drinking together. I liked him more than I'd liked any other guy, but when he enlisted in the military and announced he was headed to boot camp in San Diego, California, I was disappointed.

"You should come, too," he said. "You're always saying how much you like the ocean."

"I do," I said wistfully. "We'll see."

After he left, I discovered I was pregnant. I packed up my things and moved out to San Diego to be with Randy. I hoped he might ask me to marry him so we could raise the baby together. But when I told him I was pregnant, he was less than thrilled.

"I just enlisted in the service. You're only 18, Annie. We can't be doing this right now, having a kid. You should just have an abortion."

I bit my lip as my stomach twisted inside. The complications from my first abortion were still fresh in my mind. I was disappointed that Randy didn't want to marry me or have a baby. "You're probably right," I replied with a sigh. "I'm too young."

I went through with the abortion, but it wasn't any easier the second time around. I resented Randy for making me have it, for snuffing out a little life we could have shared and loved. He got transferred to Honolulu, Hawaii, and I returned to Nebraska, heartbroken. But after a while, I missed him, and he encouraged me to fly out and try living in Hawaii.

As I packed my things, my father stood at the door, too angry to even say goodbye. I knew what he thought: *You're always running after these losers. Why can't you just get your act together instead of making one bad decision after another?* I hardly glanced over my shoulder as I headed off.

LIKE A ROCK

I lived with Randy for a short time off base, but after a huge fight one night, I decided to move out. I didn't love him anymore and wanted to get back to the mainland. Perhaps I could get a place of my own and save until I could get enough money to go home. But rentals in Hawaii were expensive, and I wasn't sure I could afford a place on my own. My sister had lived at the YWCA; maybe I could try that, too.

"I'm moving out," I announced to Randy. "And I'm done with us."

Randy shocked me with his response. "What if we just got married?" he suggested.

Why couldn't you have suggested that in San Diego? I wanted to cry. But instead, I replied, "Sure, we could do that," as though agreeing to a casual dinner on the town.

We decided to get married in a local Catholic church and attended counseling sessions before the wedding. One evening, as we drove back from counseling, I looked out the window at the ocean and thought to myself, *If this doesn't work out, I can always get divorced later.*

Though I lived on a beautiful island surrounded by the sea, I spent the next two years in misery. I wandered around our little apartment, bored and alone, unable to call home because we didn't own a phone. Randy got transferred to Cleveland, and we moved there in 1975. After just a few months, my girlfriend back in Tacoma called.

"Will you be in my wedding?" she asked. "Please say yes!"

UNDEFEATED

I agreed to fly out for her wedding. Randy and I argued often, and I was unhappy in my new marriage. As I packed my suitcase, I had a strong feeling I wouldn't be coming back to Cleveland or to Randy. I was done.

I wrote a note to Randy before I left: *I don't know if I'll be back. I'm sorry. I just need some time to sort things out.*

I scraped up enough money to leave Randy and move to Tacoma permanently. I got a job as a waitress at a tavern and began drinking more heavily. After closing, I went out with a co-worker or a guy I'd met at the bar to drink or eat breakfast. I began sleeping around, hopping from one guy to another. After a while, I lost count of my partners. Drinking and drugs worked their way into the scene, too. I was officially reckless and out of control, but I no longer cared. My marriage had failed, I didn't have much purpose in life and I wasn't sure anyone had truly ever loved me. What did anything matter anymore?

One night, I played pool at the tavern with a seemingly nice man. After the bar closed, he invited me to coffee. "I'll drive," he suggested.

But instead of driving to the nearest coffee shop, he drove me out into a dark cornfield and raped me. I felt used and disgusting when I got home that night. I had slept with many men over the years, but I'd always had control over the situation. How could this creep have taken advantage of me like that?

I continued to date many men. When I discovered I was pregnant again, I was determined to keep the baby. I decided to move back to Nebraska; I wasn't sure if abortion was legal there but figured it wouldn't be as easy to get one there. I did not want to be tempted to make that choice again. I told my parents I was pregnant, and they were not happy.

"Again, Annie? What are you going to do?" my mother demanded.

"I'm keeping the baby this time," I insisted. "I'll find a way to make things work. I'm 23 now, not a little girl anymore."

I reconnected with a guy named Aaron I had known years before. We began dating, and I confessed that I was pregnant.

"You should get an abortion," he suggested. "If the father's all the way back in Washington, how is he gonna support you?"

"I moved here so I wouldn't have an abortion," I said firmly. "I'm not going to do it."

In 1978, I gave birth to a beautiful little girl, Kelly. Aaron immediately fell in love with the baby, and I often heard him tell my friends how cute she was as he bounced her on his knee. Unlike my past boyfriends, Aaron won the favor of my father. I hoped he might ask me to marry him, but he seemed to only love my baby, not me. I decided to date other guys, but he grew jealous and finally asked me to marry him. We wed in 1979.

From the beginning, our marriage was rocky. Aaron's older brother, who owned a sand and gravel business with him, was very controlling, and Aaron put up with his behavior. I grew angry as I saw his brother treat him so poorly.

"Why do you let him push you around like that?" I demanded. "He's being a jerk."

"He's my brother. When my dad died when I was 10, he stepped up and became the man of the house. I've always kind of looked up to him," Aaron explained.

"Well, he's not much of a role model," I retorted.

My family lived nearby, and every Friday, I brought Kelly to visit my mother and grandmother. My mother adored Kelly from the start, as did my father. My daughter's first word was "Papa." I was happy they loved my daughter but sad they had never showered that sort of affection on me.

"Isn't she a gorgeous child?" my mother marveled, kissing Kelly over and over.

"Yes, she is," I agreed. *Why couldn't you have just told me you loved me, that you were proud of me, that I was pretty? Just once?*

As Aaron's brother continued to control him, Aaron turned and tried to control me. He told me I could not work, gave me a stingy allowance for food and household items and disapproved of the few friendships I had. I made a new friend who came over to drink tea, smoke and chat with me on Monday afternoons. Our get-togethers were the highlight of my week.

"I don't want you seeing her anymore," Aaron barked at me one day. "Tell your friend to stop coming over. She's smelling up the whole house with smoke."

"Why? We're not doing anything wrong," I snapped. Why couldn't Aaron just trust me and leave me alone?

In 1981, I gave birth to our son Ben, and then three years later our youngest son, Austin, came along. For a while, things seemed to be okay. I fell into a routine as a stay-at-home mother and filled my life with kids' activities. When Aaron approached me with an idea to buy a grocery store with his brother and his sister-in-law, I was hesitant.

"Are you sure this is a good idea? Your business has been doing pretty well. Why take another risk?" I pointed out.

But Aaron went through with the plan. From the beginning, it was a disaster. I began working in the store and enjoyed visiting with the customers all day long, but Aaron fought often with his brother and soon realized he'd made a mistake. One night, I stormed out and went to the bar alone. Aaron's best friend met up with me, and we began flirting as we drank. I had never met anyone like Dave. He was sweet, funny and looked straight into my eyes when he spoke. For the first time in my life, I felt like a princess. I felt guilty about my feelings, but I couldn't deny them. For the next two years, I contemplated how I could leave Aaron to be with Dave.

In 1992, I went to an attorney and filed for divorce. One day, as I packed my things, Aaron called and told me to meet him at the school principal's office. When I arrived, I found our boys sitting there, staring up at me with wide eyes.

"So, who do you want to live with? Your mom or me?" Aaron asked them.

Ben stared at the ground. "I want to live with you, Dad."

"And Austin?" he asked.

Austin, always loyal as the baby of the family, was quiet before he spoke. "I want to live with Mom."

Tears stung my eyes. I hated to see our family torn apart, but I knew this was the price to pay for leaving my husband. I had Dave now, and I was happier with him than I'd ever been. I'd continue to be a good mother to my children, even if I could not see them every day.

Aaron later talked Austin into living with him and got full custody of the boys. Kelly, now almost 15, stayed with me. Aaron tried to keep the boys from seeing me to get back at me for my affair. I knew he was angry, but I missed my boys terribly and ached to see them.

"Don't you want to come visit Mommy?" I asked Austin over the phone one day.

"No," he shot back.

"Now, Austin, that doesn't sound like my sweet boy," I returned, fighting back tears. *What did you do to these boys, Aaron? What did you say to them? I'm still their mother!*

I married Dave in 1996. We liked to party together and decided to join a bowling league. My drinking escalated, and I began popping the beers open earlier and earlier in the day. I knew I had an alcohol problem, but I didn't know how to stop. The harder life became over the years, the more I turned to beer as my comfort and escape. I was 42 years old now; was it too late to find help?

Kelly graduated from high school that same year, and I began hearing rumors about drug use among her friends. She called me one day in tears. "We need to talk, Mom," she said between sobs.

I took her to lunch, where she continued to cry. "I have something to tell you," she whispered.

She rolled up her sleeves and showed me her wrists; they were completely purple and swollen. "I've been … shooting up meth, and think I have a vein infection or something. I'm scared, Mom."

"Oh, Kelly." I tried not to let my shock show as I inspected her skin. "We need to get you help right away."

I admitted Kelly to Valley Hope, a rehab center in Kansas. One night, I had a dream that scared me terribly. In it, I went to reach for something, and someone smacked my hand with a hard-soled shoe. I did it again, and they smacked me once more. I woke up in a panic. When I saw Kelly's counselor the next morning, I confided in her about my dream.

In my gut, I believed I knew what that dream meant. I'd been reaching for my alcohol.

One day, I saw an advertisement for a CD series on hypnosis. It claimed one could stop drinking if he or she listened to the CDs. I splurged, trading $245 for what I hoped would be the answer to my problems. As I listened to the CDs on the third day, I realized my problems were too big for hypnosis to solve. I called Dave, desperate.

"I've had it. I need help," I told him.

"Around the house? What do you mean?" he asked.

"No!" I retorted. Frustrated that he didn't understand my cry for help, I hung up.

On January 9, 2007, I went bowling with my friends. After a few beers, I hopped in the car drunk and decided to drive myself to Valley Hope. I called Kelly to tell her what I was doing.

"I can't get my act together," I told her. "I know I need help."

"We'll get you help, Mom, but you sound like you've been drinking. Turn around and go home until you're sober."

"I'm fine," I insisted.

Two blocks from the rehab facility, I heard sirens behind me. *Crap.* I pulled over to the side of the road, my pulse racing. I'd picked up two beers on the way and had just finished the last one; my breath still reeked of alcohol. I was in big trouble.

"Have you been drinking?" the police officer asked when he appeared at my window.

I gulped. "Yes, I have. I'm actually on my way to Valley Hope to check myself in."

He smiled. "Didn't quite make it, huh? Look, I'm going to make this easy on you and not give you a lecture. I just need you to get in my car, okay?"

I nodded. "Yes, sir," I said sheepishly, grateful for his kind manner.

The police officer didn't put me in a cell when we

arrived at the station but instead let me call Dave to pick me up. I dreaded the call as I picked up the phone; I knew he'd be angry with me.

When Dave arrived, he glared at me the whole way to the car. "I don't even want to hear about it, okay, Annie?" he barked. "Just shut up, and go to sleep, all right? I thought you promised not to drink when you weren't around me. Do you know how embarrassing this is, picking you up from a police station for a DUI?"

I hung my head as I climbed in the car. "I'm sorry," I said in a small voice. "It won't happen again. I'm getting help, Dave."

I checked myself into Valley Hope. A few days later, on January 13, 2007, as I sat in a family session, I had a clear vision. I saw myself reaching in a cooler for a beer, and it suddenly hit me with force. *I can't do this, but God can do this.*

I can't do this, but God can do this? Where did that come from? I felt like I'd been hit in the chest with a speeding white light. I'd sat in church many times over the years and knew about God. I'd tried inviting him into my life but had never fully understood what that meant. I knew he was love, but suddenly, sitting there in that room, I knew more than that. I knew that I needed him, that only through him true transformation would come.

That night, I cried out to God, asking him to deliver me from my alcohol problem and the destructive lifestyle I'd led for so many years. "God, I now know I can do nothing without you. I trust you with my life. Please come into my heart, and free me from the chains that have trapped me for so long. I have felt helpless for years, but I believe that with your strength, I can find hope."

Though Kelly had left Valley Hope and returned to her old lifestyle, I knew the place was just where I needed to be. I checked myself in and began attending AA classes. The teacher talked about a "higher power" that could help us, but I knew that higher power was Jesus. God had sent Jesus to earth to die on the cross for the wrong things I'd done so that I could one day live with him in heaven instead of spending eternity in hell. Jesus was the one who had pulled me from the ugly pit I'd fallen into all those years. *He* was the one who had paid the price for my sins by dying on the cross, the one who had forgiven me for the many wrong choices I'd made. Suddenly, I wanted nothing more than to grow closer to him.

I lost all desire for drinking after I invited Jesus into my life. I picked up a Bible and began to devour the pages. At first, it felt intimidating. "God, I don't really know how to read the Bible," I confessed. "I don't even know where to start."

As I prayed and wrote in a journal, God revealed certain things to me in the Bible. Each time I asked for understanding, he showed me something new. I fell in love with a verse in Matthew 5:3: "Blessed are the poor in spirit, for theirs is the kingdom of heaven." I had been a broken person, but the moment I realized I could not change without God's help, my life began to truly change.

God, I do need you. I need you every day. Thank you

for showing this to me. I know it is only because of your love, forgiveness and mercy that I am changing from the inside out.

Most nights at the center, I stayed in my room, but one night I decided to venture down to the rec room. As I headed down the hall, I passed a woman curled up in a ball outside her room. "Are you okay?" I asked softly.

She looked up, her face streaked with tears. "I don't know," she murmured.

I knelt down and talked with her for a while, then asked if I could pray for her. We became friends, and I looked forward to our time together every day after that. I thanked God that, even though I still had so much to learn, I was able to share words of encouragement with this woman.

Maybe you really can use me, God. Maybe my story will not be in vain.

ॐॐॐ

Oh, Austin, why aren't you answering your phone? Please pick up!

I set down the phone as my concern grew. My son Austin had called a few days before to announce he was going to Denver for an interview. He told me he'd rented a Harley motorcycle, which I wasn't thrilled about.

"Be careful," I'd warned him before we hung up. "Those things can be so dangerous." Ever since, I'd had an awful feeling that something might happen to him. And now, when I called to check on him, he didn't answer his phone.

Later that evening, my fears were confirmed when I got the phone call every mother dreads. "Your son has been in a serious accident. His leg has been torn to shreds, and he's most likely going to need about 30 surgeries to fix it. We're going to operate soon."

I hung up the phone, and the tears fell. Thirty surgeries? What would this mean for Austin's future? Would he be able to walk again? Would he be in pain for the rest of his life?

I had recently separated from Dave and moved to Salem, Oregon, to get into real estate after taking several online real estate courses. I lived off my 401k fund and hardly knew how I'd pay rent from month to month. A fresh start in another state had seemed like a good idea, but now, as Austin lay in a hospital far away, I felt helpless and afraid.

God, please let Austin be okay. And let me get to him as soon as possible.

Austin was transferred from Colorado to Omaha, Nebraska, for what the doctors said would be a six-hour surgery. I made the long drive, praying all the way. I'd learned that a lady had pulled out in front of Austin and ran into him. He'd ripped all the tendons and ligaments in his leg, and at the scene of the accident, his knee cap had been on his thigh, and his ankle dangled by a thread. His future was uncertain, but I knew only one thing: I needed to get to my son.

LIKE A ROCK

Two hundred miles from the hospital, I ran over a metal object in the road, and it ripped my tire to shreds. *God, what will I do now? I don't have money for new tires. I barely have enough money to get there! Please help me.*

I made it the rest of the way on my spare tire and was able to see Austin just before his surgery. His leg was up in a fixator, but he was coherent and in good spirits. "I'm praying for you," I told him, planting a kiss on his head before they wheeled him off to the operating room.

As I sat in the waiting room, I prayed and tried to remember the many comforting Bible verses I'd read. My friend had encouraged me to read the Psalms, which spoke about God as our good shepherd who watched over us in times of trouble. I knew Austin was in God's hands; I just needed to leave him there.

A guy sauntered into the waiting room as I sat there. I recognized him as one of Aaron's old friends. Sam had been pretty wild back in the day, but something seemed different about him now.

"Do you remember me?" I asked, waving him down.

"Of course. Annie. Great to see you."

"Something's different about you," I blurted.

Sam smiled. "Well, I've accepted Jesus Christ into my heart, if that's what you mean," he replied.

I smiled back. "I knew it! I have, too. I can't imagine going through this right now without him." I told him about Austin's accident, and we prayed together. He wrote his number down on a card, and I shoved it in my pocket before he left.

The doctors announced Austin's surgery had gone well. They also relayed that, contrary to what we'd first believed, Austin would not need any more surgery. *Thank you, God. What a miracle!*

I tried to decide if I should spend the money on a hotel or save my funds and go home. As I wandered outside, I couldn't remember where I'd parked my car. A woman saw my confused look and stopped me.

"Do you need help?" she asked.

"I lost my car. I don't know what I'm doing," I said. "I'm a little frazzled right now."

"Here, why don't you come with me," she suggested.

I agreed, and as I climbed in her car, I saw choir music on the front seat. *She knows Jesus!*

She told me she'd recently had surgery and asked me if I'd like to get a bite to eat. At the restaurant, I told her about running into Sam. "Two Christians in one night! God really has me covered tonight," I said happily.

"Sam?" She asked his last name and then burst out laughing. "That's my roommate's dad! What a small world!"

My new friend gave me money for tires and let me spend the night at her house. I was so grateful for God's intervention in the midst of a chaotic situation. He reminded me once again that, no matter where I went, I was never truly alone. He was always watching over me.

∾∾∾

"Annie, this is for you!" Five-year-old Jenna, my boss' daughter, came running out of the back office with something in her hand. She opened her palm and handed me a tiny rock.

"Wow, thank you, Jenna," I said, smiling. "That's so sweet of you."

I'd been a rock lover nearly all my life, and I'd had much exposure to them when Aaron was in the sand and gravel business. But since I'd come to know Jesus, I'd found new meaning in them. The Bible spoke about rocks many times. In the book of Psalms, David described God as his rock and fortress. In another part of the Bible, God performed a miracle and made water come from a rock. The more I read about them, the more I sensed God was trying to tell me something important.

I told my boss about Jenna's rock. "Annie, Jenna tells me all the time that God tells her to give people rocks so they'll know that God loves them."

"You're kidding!" Tears pricked my eyes at her words. God gave me a rock to show me he loved me! I would treasure it forever.

Later that week, I stopped at a gas station to grab a soda. As I reached for my money in my pocket, my precious rock dropped to the ground and was suddenly lost among thousands of others in the parking lot.

"Nooo!" I screamed, beginning to cry. I dropped to my hands and knees and frantically searched for it. I needed that rock!

"Can I help you look for something?" a man asked.

"Um, it's nothing," I mumbled, feeling silly. I stood to my feet. "Thanks, though."

As I drove home, tears streaming down my face, God reminded me that it wasn't the rock that was special, but the message he'd given me. He loved me!

My father passed away after a long battle with dementia. During his last days, I had a chance to be with him and tell him I loved him. I also forgave my mother for the hurt she'd caused me as a child. I hadn't felt loved growing up, but I now knew that God had been with me all along, and he had loved me, even in those moments when I felt afraid and alone.

I had struggled financially since moving to Oregon, first dabbling with real estate because I loved houses and decorating. But in a difficult economy, I decided to pursue other things. I took a job in the apartment complex where I lived. Alone in my small apartment, I began to pray about whether or not I should stay in Salem. I still loved Dave dearly and hoped we could work things out in the future. Did God want me here, or should I move back to Nebraska? Or should I venture somewhere else?

I looked up churches online and found one called Relevant Life Church. It sounded good, but I decided to check out the pastor's biography on the Web site. As I read it, a chill went up my spine.

In his biography, he stated that his favorite Bible verse was Jeremiah 29:11: "'For I know the plans I have for you,' declares the Lord, 'plans to prosper you and not to harm you, plans to give you hope and a future.'" I had heard that verse several times over the past few months and found it tremendously comforting. *I think this might be the church for me!*

I immediately felt welcomed when I walked through the doors of Relevant Life. As the pastor closed the service with a prayer, he said, "I want you to know that you are in Salem for a reason and that you are in that chair for a reason today, too."

I sat perfectly still, stunned by his words. *He's speaking right to me! This is just what I needed to hear today! This confirms that I am right where I need to be, not just in this city, but at this church.*

Though I had no friends when I first moved to Salem, I soon found a family at Relevant Life Church in the wonderful people I met. They embraced me with love, and I truly felt like I'd come home.

I continued to pray about changing jobs. One day, as I browsed the wanted ads, I stumbled upon a company called Stonemore. *I wonder if it's a concrete place,* I thought to myself. *There's those rocks again God keeps showing me!*

I applied for the job, and the company called me back for an interview. As I pulled up at the building a few days later, I realized with a chuckle that it was not a concrete place, but a cemetery! *Oh, my. I wonder what this is all about,* I mused.

But to my delight, I fit the job description perfectly. Stonemore hired me fulltime, and I was grateful for the new opportunity. I was able to reach out to many people who came through the doors, including those who were distraught over losing someone.

"I can only imagine your pain right now," I would say sympathetically. "But with Jesus, we have hope. We can spend eternity with him in heaven if we invite him into our lives, and that's the good news."

As I walked to my car one evening after work, I stopped to pick up a rock. It wasn't Jenna's rock, and it certainly wasn't anything special. But I stuffed it in my pocket, anyway, a little reminder of God's love. He'd taken my broken, messed-up life and put the pieces back together, turning them into a beautiful picture. I'd spent a lifetime looking for love in all the wrong places, but God was all I needed. *He* was my rock now.

FIGHTING
The Story of Ryan
Written by Rebekah Henwood

Something wasn't right. I had a sickening feeling about this newfound hangout spot — an old abandoned mental hospital turned construction site. The dark, gloomy shadows of the trees left an eerie sensation as I suddenly felt trapped inside the metal construction fencing which surrounded the site.

"We need to get out of here! Right now!" I yelled at my friends, but our opportunity for escape had passed. Twelve to 15 people clad in dark clothing, wearing red and blue bandanas over their faces, sped toward us full-force. Metal pieces of their knives and machetes flickered in the moonlight as I reached for the 4-inch knife I always carried in my pocket, only to realize I had left it at home. The hooded bullies quickly surrounded us, leaving no path for escape.

"Get on your knees! Get on the ground!" The young, and sometimes unsure, voices shouted commands. One of them put their hands on me. "Do it now! Get on your knees."

"I'm not getting on my knees!" I knew how to fight — I'd been doing it my whole life. I wasn't giving in without a struggle.

Someone sneaked up from behind and kicked my

knees out from under me, slamming me to the ground. They started beating me and my buddies Jake and Brad. Fists and feet slammed me in the head, back and chest, over and over.

"Give me your watch." One of the thugs nudged me with his foot.

"Seriously? You've got to be kidding me!" I fired back at him. Money was always tight, so a $5 Velcro watch was all I could afford. "Fine, if you want it that bad, go ahead, take my Velcro watch from Wal-Mart!" I took it off and slung it at him. My sarcasm didn't do me any favors.

They weren't giving up. "Give us your wallets! Give us your money!" They wanted everything.

Brad gave them everything — his wallet, flashlight and pocketknife. I wasn't budging; they were not getting my wallet! My stubbornness got me extra punches in the face.

I finally relented and pulled out my lone $20 bill and threw it at them. Sensing their anger at me, I covered my head with my hands and arms as best I could. But they managed to break my arms loose and started kicking me in the face and mouth. As I spit up pieces of my teeth to prevent choking, I was overwhelmed by a loud ringing and sharp pain in my ears. The sounds around me seemed to fade.

The gang finally retreated long enough for us to get away. I picked up Emily, sobbing, frozen by fear, threw her over my shoulder and started running. My broken ribs didn't faze me as I could see escape.

We couldn't get far enough away, so we took shelter in

a patch of sticker bushes. Since our cell phones had been stolen, Jake went looking for help. As we kept seeing the gang members run closer to us, using the flashlight they stole from Brad, we finally heard sirens and strange voices yelling our names.

I eventually came out of our hiding spot in the bushes. "Who are you?" I called out, still fearing the lurking gang members.

"I'm a police officer!"

Two busted eardrums, nine broken teeth, a few cracked ribs and a concussion later, I was finally safe.

છે છે છે

My 3-year-old ears never forgot the sound of my mom's screams coming from the kitchen that day. I could hear my stepdad, Richard, hitting her repeatedly. Rachel and Sadie held me in the living room to protect me from the scene. But I managed to get away and rounded the corner of the big refrigerator to see my mom on the floor, screaming. Her brown eyes were filled with horror and her face in a state of shock. Richard continued hitting her, his long 80s hair bouncing with every slap.

I ran up behind Richard and yanked on his pant leg with my chubby hands. "Leave my mommy alone! Don't hurt my mommy!"

Richard turned around and backhanded me to the ground. I felt so startled I froze until Rachel and Sadie ran in, scooped me up and carried me into the living room.

Though this was one of my first memories of violence in my house, it certainly wasn't the last.

Knowing we were poor defined my childhood. We lived off of food stamps and welfare, went to food banks and even had to eat at homeless shelters a few times. Mom was, for the most part, a single mom, raising four kids on her own. We lived in a beat-up trailer park in the poorest part of Graham, Washington.

Our trailer park looked rundown. Broken-down cars littered the yards of overgrown grass. Many of the neighbors used or dealt drugs. A SWAT team even invaded a neighbor's house where a lot of people got arrested. An old rusted camper trailer Mom bought before I was born took up most of our yard. Its sole purpose was to store beat-up stuff and provide a home for a bunch of bee's nests. Our front porch was falling down as the once-white wood rotted and chipped away.

The small cramped inside of the trailer smelled strongly of cigarette smoke. Mom smoked two to three packs per day, leaving the furniture and walls with a dingy yellowish tint from years of collecting smoke residue. Eric and I shared the largest room in the house — the room in between the kitchen and living room. There were no doors, which made it easily accessible to other areas of the house.

Eric and I could often be found in our room playing Sega video games on our old tiny TV. When I was about 12, Eric and I sat on my bed, roughhousing like brothers do, while playing a video game. Unintentionally, I hurt my brother. He cried for a quick minute, and we returned to playing. Before I knew what was happening, I felt my mom's open hand hitting me repeatedly on my shirtless back as I got into a ball on the ground. She didn't ask what had happened, she just started beating me.

"What is happening? What are you doing?" I managed to get out a few helpless cries.

With a cigarette in one hand, she continued hitting me, screaming, "Stop hurting your brother!"

When Mom finally stopped, she apologized, like she did every time after she abused me. "I'm so sorry, Ryan. Will you forgive me? Do you forgive me?"

I knew this wasn't really a question — it was a command. I had to forgive her or she would fly into another rage. "Yes, Mom, I forgive you."

Mom saw the hand-shaped bruise on my back her beating had left. She feared someone at school would see it and send Child Protective Services to our house. She made me wear my gym clothes to school every day for more than a week so I wouldn't have to change in the locker room.

I went through life believing physical abuse was normal, thinking all kids were disciplined by hitting and slapping and they all hid bruises under their clothes. I spent my school-age years being scared to go home because I didn't know if Mom would be mad and drag me around the house by my hair or hit me in the face until my nose bled. I dreaded that sound — the sound of her hand hitting my skin; I dreaded the sting of her slapping my face. Anger overwhelmed me every time she grabbed my hair and pulled me around the house — I felt degraded and humiliated. Yet, I didn't know it was abnormal.

I never told anyone about the abuse until after high school. I was ashamed of being poor, and I was ashamed of being beaten.

It wasn't until Mark's parents took me under their wing that I realized abuse wasn't normal, and my family life wasn't normal. Mark and I met in kindergarten and later became best friends. One of the first times I went to Mark's house, I walked into the kitchen to see Mark's mom cooking dinner — an actual legitimate meal. This was a far cry from the box of doughnuts I'd often come home to.

"Ryan, would you like to stay for dinner?" Her brown eyes were kind and warm.

"Really? You want me to stay for dinner?" I couldn't believe it!

"Yes, of course. Just let your mom know." She smiled at me sweetly. She had a peaceful aura about her that was unfamiliar, yet comforting to me.

Pretty sure Mom won't care.

That night at dinner we all sat around the kitchen table. I only remember sitting around the table at home a handful of times, on occasions like Christmas or Thanksgiving. We normally ate in front of the television or by ourselves in our rooms. Dinner at Mark's house was peaceful. There was no stress; no one cussed or screamed. Best of all, the portions were huge. I even got seconds! I was a chunky boy, and I definitely enjoyed my food. Mark's family enjoyed their food, too — probably one of the reasons we got along so well.

I spent a lot of time at Mark's house — it was a refuge for me. It was always clean and organized, unlike the chaotic mess in which I lived. His family was a second family to me. His parents treated me as their son. I went on family vacations with them: deep-sea fishing, camping and hiking. They bought me things I needed, though not without teaching me about hard work. They instilled in me a strong work ethic. When I needed new football cleats, I worked around their yard, and they bought the cleats for me.

Mark's family also took me to church. I didn't really care for church, though I did believe in God. I prayed to him out of desperation when I feared my mom. But I didn't like the church scene. I mainly went to church with Mark when there were fun activities going on.

Most significantly, I learned physical abuse was not an appropriate form of discipline. Mark wasn't a perfect kid, by any means. He screwed up many times, and he would be punished. But his parents never slapped him, beat him, screamed at him or cussed at him. They always displayed love in their actions and words.

છ્છ્છ્

The sound of my mom and stepdad screaming and swearing in the kitchen jolted me out of a sound sleep. My mom had remarried, and my new stepdad, Daniel, had just come in from his graveyard shift as the sun began its early morning rise. I sat up straight and alert as the screaming continued.

"I'm gonna do it! I can't take it anymore! I'm gonna do it!" Mom's voice had a scary intensity.

I was terrified. Mom had a long history of severe mental illness and Post Traumatic Stress Disorder as a result of being abused and molested as a child. She lived her life believing three demons were in her. She often forced me to throw away things in the house she believed were possessed with demons. Unknown to me at the time, Mom had been in and out of mental hospitals several times during my childhood. And she had attempted suicide several times.

I crept out of bed silently and slowly tiptoed to the kitchen. I entered the smoky kitchen undetected, guarded by the large refrigerator. I peeked around the corner to see Mom and Daniel sitting across from each other at the small kitchen table, two cigarettes burning in the ashtray. Mom's hair was messy, stiff from the large amounts of hairspray she used the day before. Mom had a huge bottle of her antipsychotic drugs in her hand. The second I peeked my head around the corner, Mom threw back the bottle of pills, emptying it into her mouth as she tried desperately to swallow them.

I froze in fear and shock at what my eyes were witnessing. Daniel jumped across the table, tackling Mom to the ground, grabbing her around the throat and trying to get the pills out of her mouth. I stood there, traumatized, until I saw her finally spit out the pills. There were so many. Daniel was scooping up all the wet saliva-covered pills with his hands.

Mom never saw me; she didn't know I watched her try to kill herself. I ran back to my room, threw myself under the covers on my bed and sobbed as I heard Mom crying in the kitchen. My body shook from my sobs as I mourned the instability of my family. *Who can I turn to? What should I do?*

Sadie and Rachel, who normally protected me from all the most traumatizing events in my family, were living on their own now. I didn't have them to scoop me up and carry me away from a bad situation.

As I hid under the covers, I heard Daniel pick up the phone and call Sadie. "Sadie, your mom tried killing herself. You need to get over here now!"

The 15 minutes it took Sadie to arrive felt like an eternity. The house was quiet as she came through the door. I sat up in bed and waited as the sunlight streamed through the windows. She finally peered around the corner into my room. Our eyes met, and she burst into tears as she realized I had witnessed the whole thing. She grabbed me, held me tight and cried with me. We never again spoke of Mom's suicide attempt.

Mom was headed back to the mental hospital. I began to realize this was the same place she had disappeared to several times previously. I thought back to when I was 8 years old — I woke up in the middle of the night to hear

Mom screaming. Mom often had fits because she believed demons were in the house. Once she even sent me through the house in total darkness to find the demons she felt haunting her. But that night, she was uncontrollable. My sisters kept Eric and me safely away from harm. Before Mom was taken out of the house, she begged to say goodbye to Eric and me. My sisters were reluctant, but eventually led us into Mom's dingy smoke-filled room. Her room was the worst in the house. She woke up in the middle of the night, took a few puffs and let the cigarette burn out, leaving burn marks on the carpet, sheets and furniture.

She reached out and grabbed me by my face. "I love you, Ryan. I love you. I'm sorry. Everything's going to be fine." I didn't understand what she was talking about. *What's going to be fine? Is someone going to die?* I now realized she was about to go to the mental hospital. Then she looked me right in the eyes as she said, "I'm sorry for molesting you." I didn't know what that meant, but I was scared by the whole situation and ran out of the room.

Mom said the exact same thing to Eric and my sisters. None of us can remember Mom molesting us, and we believe Mom confused her actions toward us with the traumatic events from her own childhood. Even years after her childhood, the memories of sexual and physical abuse obviously still haunted her. Perhaps these were the demons which traumatized her.

అఅఅ

FIGHTING

I couldn't remember seeing my biological dad. He was an alcoholic and left when I was about 2 years old. I could never ask Mom about Dad — a question like that would have probably sent her into a violent rage. Dad called once a year or so to talk to my sisters and me. I could never understand him; he was always drunk, and his slurred words never made any sense to me.

Because I harbored bitterness and resentment toward my dad for being absent from my life, I wasn't excited when he did call.

Dad called once while I was playing video games with some neighborhood friends. As usual, he mumbled his words, and I couldn't understand him. "Uh-huh, yeah, uh-huh." My contribution to the conversation wasn't very meaningful.

Dad could sense my lack of enthusiasm. "If you don't want to talk to me, you can just hang up any time you want and be done talking."

"Okay." *Click.* I was done. I hung up the phone and went back to playing video games.

One of my friends, whose dad had also left, looked at me with a surprised face. "Weren't you talking to your dad?"

"Yeah. I hung up on him."

"What? Why?" He seemed shocked. "If my dad called, I'd be talking to him."

For whatever reason, those words tugged on my heart. Even if Dad was a piece of crap drunkard, at least he called. I needed to give him a chance and get to know him.

He might have deserved my cold shoulder, but I didn't want to be to him what he was to me.

I didn't have Dad's phone number, so I couldn't call him back. More than a year passed before I heard from him again. At the age of 16, I had enough maturity to realize I had to take the initiative. I asked Dad if I could visit him. I had never seen my dad's face.

I made Rachel and Sadie go with me. Because they were both older than I, they had spent more time with Dad before he left, and they knew him better.

As we drove to Federal Way, Washington, butterflies fluttered in my stomach. I felt anxious, second-guessing whether I was doing the right thing.

Where do we start? I should have had 16 years with him, and now we are starting at the beginning. I'm putting in the effort here; I'm doing the work. Is this really the right thing? Yes, I need to get to know my dad.

We pulled into the parking lot of the old junky apartment complex. Dad was disabled and had lived with his brother, Chuck, for a long time. Rachel and Sadie knocked on the apartment door.

I tried to hide behind my sisters — as well as a 200-pound football player could hide behind two petite barely 5-feet-tall girls. Dad opened the door and gave the girls a hug. I walked up, and we spoke our first face-to-face words.

"Hey, Ryan."

"Hey, Dad."

We gave an awkward side hug as I walked into a dark,

musty-smelling room. I was pleasantly surprised to realize Dad was not drunk. His words weren't slurred, and I could understand everything he said.

I kept quiet at first, while Rachel and Sadie broke the ice. Dad pulled out an album with photos of his side of the family. For the first time, I heard names and saw photos of my extended family. I asked questions, breaking the awkwardness and giving Dad something to talk about. Dad's dad passed away from alcoholism. His mom was a devout Christian who died from cancer. I found out Dad had four siblings, and I had a ton of cousins who I'd never met.

Dad was a short, scrawny guy. His build was naturally small, but the years of heavy alcohol consumption, cigarette smoking and lack of proper nutrition made him appear frail. Having a completely opposite build from Dad, I joked with him about his size. Out of nowhere, he grabbed me and wrapped his arms around me in a giant bear hug. His strength surprised me for being a frail old man.

The moment seemed to freeze for a second as emotion flooded over me. That bear hug was the first real physical contact I ever had with my dad. It was the first physical display of affection I ever had from a male. I squirmed slightly from the awkwardness of the situation, but I relished the moment, not wanting it to end.

∾∾∾

UNDEFEATED

My little brother, Eric, had become a Jesus freak — a church-going, Bible-reading fanatic. My family went to church for about a year when I was a kid. Mom read the Bible sometimes, but my family and church weren't a good fit. But Eric was different now. He always wanted to read the Bible to me and tell me about things he learned, as if I was a child he could read bedtime stories to. I pretended to listen. *Just leave me alone!* I couldn't say it aloud.

During my junior year of high school, I started driving Eric to church. He went every Wednesday night and every Sunday morning. And every time I drove him to church, the conversation went the same:

"C'mon, Ryan, just try it. Just come once. You don't even know what goes on in there. Please!"

"Not today, Eric. Maybe next time."

Two year's worth of next times went by, and Eric kept asking me to join him. He sounded like a broken record.

One Wednesday night I finally gave in to his plea and joined him for Warrior Code, an all guys group. It was a laidback time of games, a message and guy talk. I breathed a sigh of relief — it wasn't as bad as I expected.

After Warrior Code, Eric introduced me to James, a Texas guy with a thick Southern drawl, who was at the church doing an internship. He invited me to stay for College Life, a group for college-aged young adults. Eric wasn't old enough to attend, but I decided to give it a shot.

Pastor Chris, who ran College Life, disproved all of my misconceptions about church. I was sure church was full of a bunch of fake people. I didn't want any part of the warm fuzzies and rainbows church people had. But Pastor Chris was different. He spoke with sincerity and passion. He wasn't fake, and I liked that. I didn't develop the same sentiments toward the other people right away, but I continued going back because I enjoyed listening to Pastor Chris.

When Pastor Chris invited me to attend Sacred Cry, a three-day conference for young adults, I didn't want to go because it cost $20. I didn't spend $20 on anything. But I bit the bullet and forked out the cash.

The speakers talked about finding healing and not allowing the damage other people caused to destroy your life or cause you to harbor resentment. I was such a rage-filled person, exhibiting my anger through frequently getting into fights. And I always thought my rage and violence was justified because of everything I went through in my life. I thought it was okay to hurt people because of how I had been hurt, physically and emotionally.

By the second day, I felt something in my heart breaking. Something inside me was longing to let go of the rage, the anger, the resentment and the bitterness. The message was about trusting God to heal the broken parts of our heart. My mind raced. *This is for me. I need healing in my life because I have been bitter and angry long enough. I want my life to change, and I want it now!* The speaker asked if anyone wanted to come to the front to be prayed for. I felt scared, but I wanted freedom from the anger and resentment that had been controlling my life for years. I knew I needed to go. James and another friend Isaac walked down to the front of the church with me.

As we reached the front of the church, I dropped to my knees and covered my chest with my hands. Despite being surrounded by about 100 people, I tuned out all the sounds in the room. It was silent. All I heard were the words James and Isaac prayed as they laid their hands on my shoulders.

I cried as I called out to God. "God, please heal me from all the things in my past. I don't want to be broken anymore! I don't want to be angry and bitter. I want it all gone. I want you, God, to take the place of all the junk in my life."

My heart broke, and all the hurt and anger spilled out as God began his work of healing. And God did it! He healed me, he changed my heart. I felt immediate relief as all the dirt in my life washed away. I wasn't angry at Mom anymore for abusing me; I wasn't angry at Dad anymore for leaving me; I wasn't angry at the circumstances that controlled my life. My happiness in life had been determined by the circumstances I was dealing with. But in that moment, I became joyful in the healing, restoration and forgiveness God gave to me.

My self-pity turned to spontaneous gratitude and real love for God. For the rest of the conference, I prayed and sang. I raised my hands in the air and danced to the music, praising God with everything I had in me. I could feel myself changing, and I wanted these changes, whatever they were. I wanted it badly. I felt excited about what God was doing — I was on a Jesus high. I was pumped up for life — my new life in which God was *the* God of my life. Like my brother, I had become the very thing for which I had made fun of him — a Jesus freak.

తతతత

Just a few months after I put my trust in God to heal me and change my life, I lay on the ground being kicked in the face by the thugs who wanted my wallet and my Velcro watch. Though God protected me during what we later found out was an Insane Clown Posse gang initiation, I seriously questioned my relationship with God. While I spent the next couple of weeks in bed licking my physical wounds, I was also recuperating mentally from a damaged sense of pride.

I just put my trust in you, God. How could you let me go through this? How could you bring this violence back into my life? I contemplated never going to church again. I was depressed and angry. I wanted to fight someone, just like the old Ryan would do.

It was time to figure out what I wanted to do with my life. I just finished two years at a community college and had made excellent grades, despite cheating and failing my way through junior high and high school. I'd wanted to be a cop since I was a kid. I had offers for scholarships to two universities, making it pretty easy to finish my bachelor's degree and proceed with a career in law enforcement.

I had friends who attended both schools, so I spent a weekend with each, exploring the college life and getting a feel for the prospective campuses. And, just like most college experiences do, my weekends included several parties as I got a taste of the extracurricular side of college life. I was vulnerable, as I questioned whether or not I really wanted to do this God thing.

The old part of me enjoyed those weekends. Drinking, dancing with girls and partying. But some new part of me felt awful after each weekend. I knew it wasn't right or smart. I knew if I went to one of these schools, I'd end up partying and become a drunkard like my dad or maybe some baby's daddy.

I was at a crossroads in my life. I wanted to go to college and get my degree. And the old Ryan definitely wanted to partake in the extracurricular things college had to offer. But I didn't know what kind of person I would be after I graduated if I did. During church one day, I cried out to God.

"God, I'm scared; I don't know what to do. I don't want to ruin my life and go down the same path as my family. Please help me! Show me what to do!"

I felt a strong pulling on my heart. God was telling me to do an internship at the church. *What? You've got to be kidding me!* The yearlong internship cost $6,000. *I'm going to turn down full scholarships for college to pay $6,000 to do an internship?*

I discussed it with Pastor Chris who was excited about the opportunity for me and got me pumped up about the

FIGHTING

idea. My mom and stepdad did not share the same sentiments. They thought I was crazy to turn down free money. But I ignored them and took the internship.

Despite my efforts to avoid the lure of the old partying stuff by doing the internship, I still managed to go down the wrong path. I was learning a lot during the internship; I was reading the Bible and growing closer to God, but my relationship with Karen, another intern at the church, created a dark cloud that hung over my life, keeping me from growing in Christ as much as I should.

Karen and I began our relationship based on lies. Interns at the church were not allowed to be romantically involved, so we lied to Pastor Chris about our relationship. I wanted to tell him about it, but Karen always manipulated me into keeping quiet. We occasionally drank together socially, and even though we never actually had sex, we did things that we knew were wrong. I felt awful. I was depressed and felt as if I would be better off dead. My life was spiraling downward out of control.

After the internship was over, we continued dating. I tried several times to end things with Karen because I knew our relationship wasn't right, but she kept begging me to take her back. When I finally ended things for good, it took more than six months for the texts and calls to stop.

After we broke up for good, I immediately felt relief, like a huge burden had been lifted. My life changed drastically. I told God I would give him the next year and devote it to him — no girls, no dating, just God. My plan worked for a while. Several friends tried to set me up with various girls, but I always ignored them.

But when my best friend, Mark, got married, I met Ruth, and I knew she wasn't someone I could ignore. Ruth was actually an acquaintance, but when she was the photographer at the wedding, I took more notice of the beautiful, tall black-haired girl. There was a sense of joy about her that was contagious and impossible to ignore. She always had a huge smile on her face. In between her capturing the memories at the wedding, we hit it off and had easy, fun conversations.

Ruth was on fire for God. She loved the Lord, and it was evident in all aspects of her life. There wasn't much for me to consider. I knew she was the one God made for me. We dated for a few months, I asked her dad for her hand in marriage and we were married five months later on July 31, 2009.

Ruth's uncle Kevin asked us to move to Salem, Oregon, for Ruth to be the youth pastor at his church, Relevant Life Church. The decision was a difficult one for me. Because of my past, I felt unqualified to be in a position of leadership or influence. *How could God really use someone with such a broken past?* But we felt this was God's calling for us, what he had uniquely made us to do at this point, so we moved to Oregon. Ruth and I shared the teaching and mentoring responsibilities, while Ruth planned activities and ran the administrative side of the youth group. God taught me that through his grace, he can use those with even the most broken pasts. And because of my past, I have been able to relate to and encourage youth living without a parent or in abusive homes. The people of Relevant Life welcomed us with open arms and loved us from the beginning, in spite of not knowing anything about me.

I wanted to be a cop for so many years. When we moved to Oregon, I applied for several law-enforcement jobs and prayed that God would open the door for the right one. I aced all the hiring tests, but I never got hired. Yet somehow, I had peace about it. God was changing my heart, and I knew he was telling me to be patient because he had something bigger in store for me. Even after I became a Christian, I thought pastors were fake. *How can they really love everybody and really care about my life?* I absolutely refused to be a pastor — I knew it wasn't for me. But Pastor Kevin encouraged me to pray about my doubt of Christian love, and God showed me that genuine Christian love means loving others as he loves us. And God changed my heart and changed my desires. I started taking classes in order to be ordained as a pastor. This is what I truly want to do with my life — what God wants me to do with my life.

෧෧෧

Several times a week, my phone rings, displaying the familiar number from the trailer in Graham, Washington, in which I grew up. Mom calls, and we talk openly about life, God and the Bible. Her abusive, suicidal and drug-using days have passed. And most importantly, our relationship has been healed and restored.

I sat across from my mom at the tiny kitchen table in her trailer one night during my internship at the church. Mom's face looked distraught, and she was fidgeting as if something was bothering her.

"I really need to talk to you, Ryan. I realized the other day that I have talked to your brother and sisters and asked for forgiveness, but I have never asked you for forgiveness."

Tears started pouring from her eyes, and she began to shake as her emotions let loose. "I really need to ask you if you have forgiven me already, and if you haven't, if you will forgive me for what I did to you in your childhood?"

I felt relief and a strange happiness that she acknowledged what had happened during my childhood. We rarely talked about those years, but when it did come up, she always denied all the horrible things she did. "It wasn't really that bad," she'd say. It was liberating to hear her admit, "You had a screwed-up childhood, and I am sorry."

I looked her in the eyes. "Not only have I forgiven you, but I forgave you a while ago." I shared with Mom what happened at Sacred Cry. "Mom, God healed me! He got rid of the anger and resentment in my life. This is real — I really believe this." I poured out my testimony and how God had changed my whole life.

"Mom, I really want to move past this."

She looked at me in shock, as if she couldn't believe I

was able to forgive her and let go of the anger and resentment.

It was a scene I had dreamt about for years. And God made it a reality. He changed my heart enough to forgive my mom and, in turn, gave me the opportunity to witness to her and share the love of Jesus with her. After years of pain and abuse, I am only strong because God restored me.

We shared tears and shared hugs. "I love you, Mom."

"I love you, too, Ryan."

THE STENCH
The Story of Rhonda Reich
Written by Angela Welch Prusia

Unaware of the deadly explosion of red blood cells within me, I leaned over the tub and lathered Maddie, the family Westie. The metal track of the shower door pressed into my chest, so I shifted my weight. The nasty scab on my knee made kneeling awkward.

"You're a dirty pup today," I said to Maddie as I scrubbed dingy white fur. Rivers of soap suds ran down her back and swirled down the drain. Oatmeal-scented shampoo overtook the stench of wet dog.

I adjusted the temperature and sprayed Maddie with the hose, completely ignorant of the internal war waging under the veil of my skin. Hidden within a vein, a massive blood clot dislodged and sped toward my heart.

"Look at you." I continued my one-sided conversation. A drenched Maddie gazed up at me with pleading eyes.

"Almost done." I grabbed her towel and grinned at her pathetic dog act. She was as bad as my two kids when they had chores.

My grasp loosened with my awkward position, and she wiggled free.

"Ugghh." I shielded my face when Maddie shook, but it did little to stop the deluge of water flying off her fur.

"Thanks," I grunted, toweling us both off.

Maddie trotted down the hall after I finished blow drying and brushing her. For a small dog, she had a big dog attitude. My knee throbbed as I stood, and my breath caught when my chest suddenly tightened.

Unseen to me, the clot passed through my heart and burst into my lungs, clogging both lobes with smaller masses of red blood cells. I brushed aside the chest pain and continued with my normal chores. My husband, daughter Sydney and son Trenton had gone to a family reunion in Montana, and I relished some time alone.

The silent countdown began. Death waited in the chambers that expelled my every breath. And I was oblivious.

৵৵৵

I felt horrible the next day, but I forced myself to go to work at my job with the Department of Administrative Services for the State of Oregon. With the weekend hours away, I gave myself a pep talk. "You can tough it out, Rhonda. Tomorrow you can sleep."

Saturday morning, however, extra sleep eluded me. The pain had increased, making it difficult to get comfortable. Even my breathing was labored. I lay in my bed and thought back to the last weekend of July when I had my bout with the waterslide. My wipeout resulted in a knee injury and pulled hamstring.

The Splash Bash at Relevant Life Church where my husband worked as the lead pastor promised loads of fun, especially with temperatures in the high 90s. The smell of hot dogs sizzling on the grill and colorful inflatables enticed people on the street to join in the entertainment. Our normal Sunday morning attendance doubled in just one afternoon.

I volunteered most of the afternoon, helping kids and making sure everyone played safely. Sweat dripped down my back after the second hour, and I eyed the nearby waterslide with its two parallel runs for racing. Laughter peppered the air as kids flopped onto their bellies. Momentum propelled them forward, spraying water droplets into the air.

"Yes! I won!" someone would scream.

Another kid would jump off the slide and wiggle a wet bottom in a silly victory dance.

I couldn't wait for a chance to get soaked. The minutes dragged by until my shift finally ended and I could kick off my flip flops. I hurried to get in line, careful not to take out a kid in my exuberance.

"Wanna race?" I asked a friend opposite me.

She took off in answer and beat me to the slide.

"Hey, wait for me!" I raced toward my side.

Cra-a-ck!

A couple feet from the inflatable, my ankle gave out.

Boom!

I skidded across the parking lot, sprawling awkwardly in front of an audience of friends. Their groans met my ears. My face, pink from the sun, flamed red hot.

"Are you okay?"

"Can you walk?"

Voices of concern surrounded me.

Pain shot through my body, tempered only by my humiliation. Asphalt shredded my right knee to hamburger.

"Let's get you cleaned off," Lisa, a CNA in our church, offered.

I hobbled inside the building with the help of her and several others.

"I feel like such a klutz," I mumbled. My left hamstring throbbed.

"It happens to everyone," Lisa encouraged as she cleaned up my scraped toes and raw knee. The band aids in the church office hardly covered the wound.

Now, three weeks later, I didn't correlate my current pain and shortness of breath with my injury on the waterslide. Otherwise healthy, I was not one to visit the doctor much.

I pulled myself out of bed and turned on the computer. I keyed in my symptoms and ended my Google search with a self-diagnosis. I rationalized my pain as a bruised chest wall from leaning over the tub with the dog. A blood clot never entered my thoughts.

❧❧❧

A knock sounded at my door. Trenton's best friend, Alex, arrived to work. With Trenton gone for the week, Alex came to help move firewood as payment for summer camp fees. Several cords of wood needed to be moved off our driveway and stacked in piles on the side of our home for the cold winter months.

"Hey, Pastor Rhonda," Alex greeted me.

We talked a few minutes, but I could tell he was anxious to get started.

"You can use the wheelbarrow to move the wood," I explained and watched as he began.

A hardworking young man, Alex didn't have the experience my son did with the job, so I loaded a second wheelbarrow to save time.

I grabbed some work gloves and Ibuprofen. Bruising took time to heal, so I was just going to have to put up with the discomfort and shortness of breath. If I wanted the work done before nightfall, Alex needed help.

"It's a hot one." I swiped at the perspiration which rolled down my face.

Alex took a gulp of water and agreed.

I pulled a stool next to the shrinking pile of wood in the driveway. The heat added to my misery, but I refused to quit. Instead, I leaned on the stool and loaded more wood for Alex to haul and stack.

He could see my pain, but neither of us knew how close death lurked.

෧෧෧

I suffered through the next week of work like a stubborn child. I reasoned that if I could push past the out-of-breath feeling, I'd get a second wind. My husband was upset when we talked on the phone.

"Why don't you go to the doctor?" he asked.

"I'm fine," I said, brushing aside his worry.

He wasn't convinced.

"You and the kids are picking me up Friday after work. I'll rest then," I promised. We were headed to a friend's vacation home in Central Oregon; surely I'd feel better after a week.

Saturday morning dawned sunny and cool, so my daughter and I took Maddie for a walk around the property while Trenton and Kevin took off for the Little Deschutes River. I told my husband I would take it easy; I didn't even bother with makeup or fixing my hair.

Gravel crunched beneath our feet as we walked past several homes and undeveloped lots. Getting away from the valley was always a treat, even if the mosquitoes were making a meal of me. Closer to the river, the trees got thicker. The scent of pine filled the air.

"I'm going to pick up the pace on the way back," I told Sydney. Even after walking almost a mile, I still felt winded. It was time to kick this thing and get back in shape.

If she said something, I didn't hear her response. The world suddenly went black.

Terrified cries lifted the fog surrounding me. "Dad!" Sydney screamed for help somewhere in the distance.

My eyelids fluttered open, and I found myself lying in the dirt. My tongue rolled across my lips and tasted the same dust which covered my shorts and t-shirt. My daughter never panicked; hearing her made me realize something might really be wrong with me.

"Deep breath." I forced down my fear and managed to pull myself up and brush off the debris.

Underbrush cracked as my family hurried toward me, but I was too winded to call out. A nearby electrical box provided support.

"Mom!" Sydney rushed up to me with her father and brother in tow. Her breath came heavy. "Are you okay? You passed out, and I couldn't wake you."

Kevin didn't wait for the details. "I'm getting the Durango." He raced off and returned in minutes. Anxiety lined his face. "You're going to the hospital. Now."

ॐॐॐ

My symptoms ignited a rush of activity at the hospital. A nurse took one look at me and told me to take a seat. "Clear Room 4," she barked.

Despite the full waiting area, I was given top priority. The attention made me even more nervous.

"Have you ever been hooked up to an EKG machine?" a technician asked.

I shook my head as he placed electrodes on my arms, legs and chest.

"These will send impulses here," he pointed to a machine, "which will trace the activity in your heart."

Not long after, a woman dressed in a lab coat entered

the room and introduced herself as my doctor. Her confidence put me at ease. "Your heart looks good," she said as she read the results. "But in the emergency room, we need to rule out the worst case scenarios first. Based on your symptoms, I need to check that you don't have a pulmonary embolism."

Kevin and I exchanged a look. *How bad could it be?*

The doctor ordered a CAT scan, so I was ushered into the radiology room. Because of my allergy to iodine, the dye which would show areas of concern, a steroid and Benadryl were administered as well.

Panic gripped me when my heart began to race.

"That's normal," the technician reassured me, but the whole experience was beginning to unnerve me.

Back in the E.R., the doctor stared at the results in a stupor. Three-fourths of my lungs showed blockage from a pulmonary embolism.

"I wouldn't mess with your wife," she addressed Kevin. "She's one tough cookie."

I would've smiled, but her next words stopped me cold.

"Quite frankly, I don't know how you're alive, Rhonda."

I blinked in disbelief. I was 47.

"The CAT scan clearly indicates you have a massive bilateral pulmonary embolism," the doctor continued. "You passed a very large blood clot that somehow broke apart for the fragments to have filled most of your vessels of both lungs in this way."

THE STENCH

I clung onto each word, trying to make sense as she explained what could cause a clot of this size. *I was healthy. How could this happen?*

"That's why you've had trouble breathing," she explained. "Thankfully the embolism didn't stop your heart. But how you've endured for eight days is beyond me."

Fear churned my thoughts, and I shuddered as reality hit. *What if Trenton's friend Alex had witnessed my collapse? What if I'd died alone? How long till Kevin and the kids found me?*

Death's cold breath prickled the hair on my skin. I was a walking miracle.

࿓࿓࿓

Treatment beat the alternative, but injecting myself with an anti-coagulate three times a day marred my stomach with bruises. To keep my blood levels in the target area, I had to undergo regular testing. Brain bleeds and injury were a constant threat, and progress was slow. Two and a half weeks passed before I breathed normally. My medicine left me with a sickly feeling, and I gained 40 pounds because exercise and the Vitamin K in green vegetables messed up my blood levels.

"It's fortunate you were near Bend when you passed out," my family doctor confided in me on our return home. "St. Charles Hospital is known for its trauma care."

I breathed a prayer of gratitude.

The months of September, October, November and December were filled with visits to specialists — a pulmonologist, an allergist and hematology oncologist. Large chunks of my day disappeared at clinics and hospitals while I gave vials of blood for tests I could barely pronounce. I even participated in a sleep study — anything and everything to determine the underlying cause of my blood clot.

The ultrasound on my right leg never showed evidence of a clot. The specialists wanted to be on the offensive, lessening the chance of future problems, but they were stymied. I never thought to mention my pulled hamstring, so an ultrasound was never ordered on my left leg.

As a pastor's kid and preacher's wife, I hadn't strayed far from my Christian faith. I'd spent seasons going through the religious motions, but never had my faith been so tested.

"Why me, God?" I cried out, wishing for answers. "Why did you spare me?"

Did I survive the embolism because I had cancer or some other life-threatening condition that would now be revealed?

One minute I believed God was in control.

The next minute my faith crumpled under my own doubt. The whys made me crazy.

Sometimes people assume pastors know all the answers, but we have our questions, too. I wrestled with God as I tried to make sense of my new physical limitations. No matter how hard I pushed, the matches revealed his presence in new ways, and I felt drawn to my maker.

Nothing surprised him. My brush with death revealed my own lack of control. I was both humbled and amazed to know he took care of me, even when I walked in the dark.

లల

One test involving viper venom began to reveal answers. After months of waiting, I tested positive for Lupus Anticoagulant Disorder, a disorder with an abnormally high risk of blood clotting.

The news was bittersweet. Finally I had an answer. But the answer made my heart sink. I would spend the rest of my life in and out of hospitals, dependent on blood thinners to keep me alive.

On my way to work, two blocks from church, I broke down in my car hearing the radio play "That's what Faith Can Do" by Kutless.

I'd heard the song a dozen times, but this day, every phrase resonated on the cords of my heart.

Even when the sky is falling
I've seen miracles just happen
Silent prayers get answered.
Broken hearts become brand new
That's what faith can do.

The same Jesus who rose from the grave had power over all sickness and disease. Encouraged by the song, I began to pray fervently for healing.

Jesus could heal me regardless of my actions, but there is something about faith that touches his heart. He'd already shown me his protection when I was oblivious; now he wanted my unwavering belief in his power.

⇜⇜⇜

Two months after my diagnosis, my doctor ordered a retest. With something as serious as Lupus Anticoagulant Disorder, it was standard procedure to retest patients before long-term treatment.

"I don't understand." My doctor gaped in amazement when the results came back. I sat up straighter on the exam table.

"Occasionally we'll get a false positive." Confusion laced the doctor's tone. "But this is incredible. There is no evidence of the disorder."

Tears welled up in my eyes. I knew the result wasn't a false positive. God had answered my prayer.

The doctor had no other explanation.

But I knew. I was healed. I hurried to call my husband, my mom and friends — everyone who'd joined me in prayer for healing.

Only God could've worked something so miraculous.

⇜⇜⇜

THE STENCH

Fast forward a year.

"You need to pray." My co-worker looked grave the day before Thanksgiving. "My sister's at the hospital because she had a stroke."

A familiar rush of compassion swelled within me. My own suffering brought a level of empathy to those with long-time sickness that I hadn't known before. Like those in our church who needed prayer, I didn't take the request lightly. I'd walked in their shoes, so I knew the frustration of scheduling my days around doctor visits and the endless wait for test results. My prayers became real cries from my own experience.

When I returned to work after the holiday, my co-worker stopped me. "My sister's not doing well. She had two smaller strokes and tested positive for anti-something."

"Lupus Anticoagulant Disorder?" I paled, the words bringing back a flood of emotion.

More details made my heart hurt for this young woman who desperately wanted to be a mom. I felt like a soldier spared from the same battle which took the life of his buddy. Knowing I was spared spurs me to live purposefully — not just going through the motions like I often lived before.

☙ ☙ ☙

Kevin and I recently talked after he returned from a four-day fact-finding trip to Haiti with 14 other pastors.

UNDEFEATED

Almost two years after the 2009 earthquake hit the country, the devastation continues to be daunting. Convoy of Hope, a faith-based ministry dedicated to disaster response and feeding the hungry, wants to form partnerships between churches and orphanages and schools to feed 100,000 kids per day for the next year and provide education so the children can change the future.

"I can't believe what I saw," my broken husband confessed. "I've never cried so much in my life, and we were only on the ground 28 hours."

He related stories of shattered lives and streets littered with rubble.

"Six hours on the ground, and I wanted to come home."

I raised my eyebrows in surprise.

My husband loved bringing the good news of Jesus to difficult places, having visited Honduras and many countries in Africa.

"It's the hardest place I've ever traveled." Kevin told me about a visit to one orphanage founded by a young Haitian lawyer who happened upon a case of kidnapping soon after the earthquake. "The place served 64 kids, and it was filthy."

Sadness tugged at my heart.

"I was assaulted by the smell of urine and dirty bodies," he said. "Kids ran around naked except for a t-shirt. And the lot was scattered with rubble. I even saw a hog roaming freely in the trash."

Images of garbage heaps filled my mind.

THE STENCH

"The stench was so awful, I wanted to hurl." Kevin hung his head in shame. "I kept wondering what I could offer in so short a time. Wouldn't it be better to send money?"

My husband's vulnerability touched me. *What could any of us offer in our short time on earth?*

"I watched the kids hang back because none of us pastors stepped forward." Kevin's eyes brimmed with tears. "But then I felt God whisper to my heart, and I picked up this little boy who was naked except for a red t-shirt." He smiled. "He was fascinated with seeing pictures of me and him on my digital camera screen."

I remembered pictures Kevin had shown me of dirty faces with big smiles.

"A swarm of kids surrounded us as soon as I reached out. Everyone wanted to be held." My husband sighed as the memory brought back raw emotions. "Our hugs meant more than the candy we brought. Just a tiny drop of affection made these kids glow."

The two of us sat in silence, both lost in our thoughts.

"We left the orphanage, and I could still smell the acrid odor of urine on my sleeves," Kevin said, breaking the quiet. "I couldn't stop crying as we bounced along the rough road leading away. 'God,' I prayed, 'help me never forget the stench of lost humanity.'"

My husband's words sank deep within my spirit. "That's why we're here," he said as much to himself as to me. "To spread the hope of Jesus to those who are without him."

Kevin's right. God alone knows the number of my days, and I don't have time to waste. I need to live each day with purpose. Around me, people reek of pain and brokenness. God doesn't want me going through religious motions. He wants me to bend down and pick up the hurting — immerse myself in the stench of messy lives, pointing people to Jesus, our only hope.

Only then comes true healing.

LOSING THE FIGHT, WINNING THE BATTLE
The Story of Todd
Written by Marty Minchin

Dinner was progressing normally, if you call what could happen around our table normal. Dad sat on one end, my stepmom on the other. As the oldest, I had one side of the table to myself and faced my two brothers. The waning afternoon light filtered in through the window behind me, warming my back.

The stilted conversation came to an abrupt halt when one of my brothers passed gas.

I clapped my hand over my mouth to hold in a giggle, but little was funnier to a first-grade boy. My younger brothers' shoulders shook as they chuckled over the dinner faux pas.

Dad's gaze passed over each of us as he silently selected a culprit. Faster than a flyswatter, his arm shot out from his chest, and he backhanded me across the face.

Flesh slapped flesh, and the force of Dad's blow catapulted me off the seat into the window. My head crashed through the glass. The window shattered into shards on the ground outside, and after taking a few seconds to absorb the shock, I gingerly pulled my body back into the dining room. I reached back to check on the cut and felt a warm, sticky substance on my fingers. My family stared at me in silence. *The blood. I need to wash it off.*

I sprinted out the door and down the driveway, running right by the creek nearest to the house on our 2-acre farm. *I've got to get away, get out of here where they can't see me.*

Across the meadow was a second creek, and as I ran closer, the sound of the burbling water soothed the hurt and rage in my soul. I crouched down on the bank, running my hand in the cool water and dipping my palms full to clean my head wound.

The minutes passed, and no one came to check on me. No voices called across the meadow. I sat small and alone amidst the tall trees and rambling meadow. *Do they care where I went? Didn't they see that I have a gaping cut on the back of my head?*

The blood stopped about the time I had mustered up the courage to walk back to the house. I took my seat at the table, and we carried on as if nothing had happened.

రావురావురావు

By the time I was 6 years old, I had lived in four foster homes. My mom, who I never lived with, had five kids from several men. When she and my dad divorced, she couldn't afford to raise all of us. My younger brother, Sam, and I lived with an aunt for a while before we were shuffled through foster homes. All of my foster parents took us to church, where I learned plenty of Bible stories but nothing about how to handle the abuse that my dad had in store for us.

My biological dad put our family back together after he married my stepmom, Rose. Raised Catholic, she was an Irish beauty with fiery red hair. She was only 19, just 13 years older than me, and she could pass as my sister. She brought a son, younger than Sam, to our blended family. It was the 1960s, and while most girls her age were out having fun, Rose was raising three boys and shouldering her share of the abuse Dad regularly meted out to the family. He had no problem hurting her right in front of us. Once he kicked her in the backside so hard it broke her tailbone.

Dad didn't raise us with the rod. He raised us with his fist. From the start I saw him as a hairy, brawny monster that came home from the tavern with a gut full of alcohol and a mind bent on cruelty.

The sound of him downshifting his 1965 Ford van as he pulled into the driveway would send my anxiety level skyrocketing. His voice boomed through our farmhouse, which he inhabited like a troll ruling over his cave. No matter how hard I tried to please him, the slightest misstep could unleash his brutality.

Rose, who I still call Mom, was kind. While she and Dad didn't go to church, she would rouse my brothers and me out of bed on Sundays and take us to children's programs at a nearby house of worship. She taught me that no matter how bad it got, if I stood strong, I'd win in the end.

ৡৡৡ

Dad had that look in his eye as soon as he walked in the front door. "Boys, outside. Now."

We knew what was coming, but we knew better than to argue or run. He was the giant, and in my story, I was no David with a slingshot full of pebbles ready to take down Goliath.

Sam and I silently walked out to the meadow, Dad's heavy footsteps trailing behind us. We stopped at the electric fence and removed our shirts and shoes. This was part of the routine. Dad's violence knew no bounds, but he was wily enough to know that if he left marks on us, the Department of Child Protective Services might take us away. This particular torture at the fence was designed to hurt us on the inside.

"Arms up," Dad ordered.

We obediently raised our arms while Dad wound a wire around our waists and connected it to the fence. Our bare feet served as a ground, and the electricity pulsed through my slender body. It started as zaps and grew into excruciating throbs. The waves of electricity almost had a heartbeat of their own.

The pain was too great for us to form words, and our screams carried uselessly across the field.

"You're out in the country, who's going to hear you?" Dad sneered. "Just scream."

So we did, but after a few minutes, our yowling got on his nerves.

LOSING THE FIGHT, WINNING THE BATTLE

"Just shut up."

That order was easy to follow. By this time we were somehow used to the jolts of electricity wracking our bodies. Besides, escape was impossible.

At least today Dad left the water hose coiled on the ground. Sometimes he liked to wet our feet while we were being electrified and watch us dance.

I repeated my silent vow to myself when we finally were allowed to trudge back to the house.

When I have a family, I will never treat them like this.

☙☙☙

One of Dad's favorite sayings was that if we didn't play ball with him, we couldn't play ball with anyone.

That philosophy worked for me. As long as I did my chores on the farm, Dad would let me do things outside our home. Pleasing and appeasing became my modus operandi; in return, I took every opportunity to stay away from the house. Dad was easily angered, and home was never safe for me.

As a child, Royal Rangers at church — an organization similar to the Cub Scouts — was my out. In high school I joined the football and wrestling teams and played drums in the pep band and the jazz band. I savored the hours without Dad supervising my every move.

But Dad didn't let up when I was at home, and by age 18, I was nearing the end of my tolerance.

When Mom and Dad went out for dinner one night

that autumn, I used the rare moment of privacy to call a girl I had my eye on at school.

"Hey, Todd, who're you talking to?" Brett, Rose's son and my stepbrother, stuck his head into my bedroom.

I cupped my hand over the mouthpiece.

"Get out," I hissed, frantically motioning him to shut the door. "Go away."

"C'mon, Todd. Is it a girl?" His mocking tone infuriated me. "Is that a GIRL on the phone? Todd's got a girlfriend!"

"I'll call you right back," I told the girl as calmly as I could, then set down the receiver to give Brett a piece of my mind and maybe a piece of my fist.

I found the little weasel in the laundry room trying to hide.

"Didn't you see I was on the phone? I can't even get five minutes of privacy around here without you bugging me. When I'm on the phone, you need to leave me alone until you hear that receiver click. Got it?"

He didn't care one way or the other about what I was saying, but I figured a little brotherly punch would show him I was serious.

My timing couldn't have been more disastrous. Just as my fist connected with Brett's shoulder, the outside door swung open. Mom and Dad were home from dinner. My blow wasn't hard, but Brett collapsed dramatically between the washer and the dryer.

All Mom saw was her 15-year-old baby lying on the floor. All Dad saw was the kid he had specifically asked me to look out for at school hurt by my hand. It was all too obvious that Dad's protective order also applied to our house.

"We'll take care of this in the morning."

His meaning was clear. I'd pay for this tomorrow.

❧ ❧ ❧

There was no tomorrow.

"Come get me," I told my friend on the phone that night. "Now. I'm out of here for good."

My thoughts were blurred with the images of the horrors Dad might conjure up for me tomorrow. Even though my friend lived only seven miles away, it was far enough for me to start my own journey in life.

I dropped out of high school one semester short of graduating and got a job as a fireman. I'd worked as an apprentice fireman since I was 16, and I loved it. I moved into an apartment with my older brother in St. Helens, and after growing up on the farm, this town felt like a big city.

Dad and Rose never called once to find out what had happened to me or where I had gone. It was baffling.

My biological mom lived in St. Helens, and now that I was on my own, I was free to reconnect with her. I'd stop by a lot to play basketball with her son, who was my half-brother.

A high school girl who lived down the street drove by my biological mom's house all of the time on her way in and out of the neighborhood, and it wasn't long before we were talking. When I joined the U.S. Army and moved to Alabama, Sharon and I stayed together, even though we lived thousands of miles apart.

Sharon graduated from high school and started college, but we were tired of the separation. She agreed to transfer to a school in Alabama, but we needed to talk to her mom first.

Her mom had a more practical solution.

"Why don't you just get married?" she asked us as we sat in her living room during my two weeks of leave.

That made sense to me. I dropped down on one knee right there and asked Sharon to marry me. There was no question about her answer, and within a week we were husband and wife. By the end of my leave, we had bought a car topper, filled it with everything we owned and were on the road to Fort Rucker, Alabama, to begin our married life.

☙☙☙☙

I had my first — and for a long time, my only — drink at age 13 on a hunting trip with my dad. It was the only hunting trip we ever went on together.

We headed into the woods and ran into a friend of Dad's who somehow had loaded what seemed like an entire refrigerator's worth of drinks into the back of his truck. His cooler brimmed with beers and whiskey.

"Want a drink, son?" my dad asked.

LOSING THE FIGHT, WINNING THE BATTLE

"Sure." *Why not,* I thought.

Dad reached into the cooler and handed me an amber bottle filled with Sunny Brook Whiskey, the condensation running down the sides of the cold glass. I took a slug, wincing as the burning liquid flowed down my esophagus. After the tortures I endured at home, I had no problem handling the sting of liquor. I downed half the bottle that night and passed out. I have no recollection of the rest of that trip. That my dad allowed a 13 year old to drink that much is unthinkable.

I didn't drink again until Sharon and I began to frequent the enlisted men's club at a base in Alaska, which I was transferred to five months after our wedding. I had always loved music, and at the club we could listen to live bands and have a drink. Sometimes we'd invite our single friends who lived in the barracks over to our townhouse, and we'd play music and party.

Sharon and I thought we were living the American dream. We were both working, and we had a place of our own and could pay our bills. We had lots of friends, and we liked to have a good time with them.

My wife came from a strong religious background, and we attended church regularly. From my understanding of the Bible, it was fine to drink as long as you didn't get drunk. I'd drink a few beers at a tailgate party before a football game or have a couple of drinks at a Christmas party. Alcohol never made me lose control, and from a religious standpoint, I didn't think I was doing anything wrong.

UNDEFEATED

෴෴෴

Sharon gave birth to our daughter, Carys, in 1986. Her birth made me re-evaluate everything about my life. I didn't want to raise my children in a military family, and it was time for us to live a "normal" life. It also was time for me to slow down on my drinking, and I cut way back.

We moved to Salem, Oregon, and I took a job with my brother-in-law's beer distributing company. I drove a beer truck for a year, then worked at a cabinet factory. I loved how the plywood entered the factory in sheets and left as cabinets. Unfortunately that job didn't pay enough to support my family, so in 1991, I took a job with the Department of Corrections.

Walking into the penitentiary was like entering a burning building every day. Once the heavy front door slammed behind me, I'd have to survive eight hours trapped inside with whatever violence, noise and resistance the 2,000 inmates could throw at us. We moved inmates around the prison, and the uncooperative men would fight violently against us. To extract an unwilling prisoner from his cell, several of us would don football gear and riot helmets before entering. The noise in the prison could be deafening as cuss words and angry screams bounced off the gray walls. Sometimes after work I would sit in my truck with the music cranked up to drown out the sounds from the workday that stayed in my head.

Home had its own set of problems.

LOSING THE FIGHT, WINNING THE BATTLE

I had wanted to be a dad so badly, but I had no idea how to be one. The only example I had grown up with was what *not* to do.

Carys was a headstrong, social child. Among our family and friends in Salem, she was the youngest child, the Shirley Temple and the constant center of attention. She became bold and empowered. By age 4, she was performing in talent shows. She was extremely smart and an old soul, intelligent beyond her years. I thought I was providing her with the loving environment I craved as a child.

In her early years, Carys behaved when she was around Sharon or me. But when she was out of sight, whether it was a Sunday school class at church or kindergarten, the trouble began.

We got our first inkling of Carys' behavior problems at her kindergarten parent-teacher conference. Sharon and I sat slack-jawed as the teacher explained our daughter's disruptive behavior. Carys giggled in class. She chattered to her classmates when she should have been listening.

"What are you talking about?" I finally asked the teacher. Could this child she was describing really be our daughter? "She doesn't talk that way."

The teacher tried to be gentle.

"Let me give you an example," she told us. "When our class was lining up to leave the library this week, Carys didn't want to go. I asked her to join the line, but she climbed on the table instead and refused to get down. She was pretty loud about it. I had to have another teacher physically remove her from the table and carry her out of the library."

What? Our Carys would never act like that.

But she did. By second grade, we were meeting with counselors. In third grade, she regularly brought home notes from the teacher. I tried reasoning with her. I tried making her sit on her bed to think about her behavior. I never hit her, but I used the voice inflections I'd picked up as an Army sergeant to make her cringe. It was never enough to make her change.

The only thing I didn't do was fully hand over the situation to God. I asked him for help, but I believed I had the tools to fix it myself.

అఇఇఇ

By 1999, Sharon and I were seeing a counselor for guidance in dealing with Carys. The counselor had us draw up a list of 10 things Sharon and I would hold Carys accountable for. One of those was taking the garbage out to the curb for the weekly pickup. Every other week she also would need to take out the recycling bin.

"Carys, don't forget that tomorrow is garbage day," I reminded her one evening on my way out the door to the bowling alley. "The recycling can goes out, too."

She murmured an acknowledgement, and I left pleased with the gentle way I had handled the situation. We could check this responsibility off the list for this week.

I spotted only one can on the street when I pulled

around the corner a few hours later. *Where's the recycling can? I told her to put it on the curb, too!*

The incident uncapped the bottled-up rage inside me, and the anger rushed into every corner of my being. *How could she disobey so blatantly? It was such a simple task!*

I swung open the front door and marched down the hall of bedrooms in our ranch house. Carys' room at the end of the hall was dark. Sharon followed behind me like a shadow.

"Get up, Carys." I kept my voice under control. "You need to take the recycling out. Then you can go back to bed." I flipped on the overhead light to wake her up.

She pushed her legs out of bed and padded toward the door. I put my hand on her elbow and escorted her to the garage.

"What's going on?" Sharon asked. "Why are you doing this?"

My wife kept talking, but I tuned her out. Carys needed to take out the recycling right now.

As the garage door whirred up, Sharon pushed around us and planted herself in the path to the recycling can.

"What are you doing, Todd?" she demanded.

The world closed around me, and through a tunnel of clarity, I could only see Carys, the recycling can and the street. Sharon was in the way. I reached out my arm to push my wife aside so I could walk around her. The rage I was laboring to constrain shot into my arm like a pulse of energy, and with the strength of a video game character, I threw Sharon across the garage like a rag doll.

She crumpled to the floor, and the trance of my rage was broken. I had become the man I most wanted not to be: my dad. That night, I crossed my own line.

❧❧❧

Sharon wasn't physically injured, but our marriage broke that night. I slept at a friend's apartment, and the next morning I enrolled in an anger management class, hoping the horror of that night would dissipate. But when Sharon immediately filed for divorce, I didn't fight her. I didn't trust myself anymore.

We also had a son, Patrick, who had been born in 1996. Since I worked the graveyard shift at the penitentiary, he stayed with me during the day while Sharon worked and Carys was at school. That connection maintained a rapport between Sharon and me. I didn't believe in divorce, so when she asked me to move back in a year later and give our marriage another go, I readily agreed.

The old problems lingered, though, and in some cases had grown. Carys was a year older and a year smarter, and her disobedience now bordered on disrespect. Our marriage fell apart the first time because of my inability to deal with my daughter — I hadn't learned any new parenting skills during the separation.

Sharon and I tried to work it out, even taking a family vacation to San Antonio. Soon after we returned, I took Patrick with me to visit a friend who sold ammunition that I needed for my hunting rifle. The guy was a gun dealer and had a shooting range in his basement, and Patrick listened, enthralled, for 45 minutes while my friend described guns and shooting safety. As a reward for his attention, the guy said Patrick could try out one of his handguns.

Patrick was only 5, so I held the small-caliber handgun while he pulled the trigger. My son was delighted. My wife was incensed when he told her.

That was the end of our marriage. She told me to get out, and I did as soon as I bought a house on the other side of town. I had given this marriage everything I could, and I wasn't going to try again.

కావికావికా

All I had ever wanted was a family. I had cut both of my kids' umbilical cords and held them in the hospital before their mom did. I changed diapers and washed bottles. I loved being a dad. I was awash in loneliness without my kids, and I started drinking heavily. I kept it under control if Patrick was over at my house, but otherwise I could put away as many as 30 beers a day.

I eventually joined an online dating site, where my code name was BIGDUCKSFAN after my love of the University of Oregon football team. Janet was a big sports fan herself, and we connected over the Internet. Our first phone call turned into a three-night talking marathon over one weekend. We had so much in common. She was a nurse and worked the graveyard shift like I did. She was from Oregon, but her brother had attended my high school, where he and I had been friends. We had aunts and uncles with the same names.

When God closes one door, he opens another one.

Janet and I agreed to meet for the first time at a park. We talked and walked around that park for three hours, our intrigue with each other growing. As the sun set, I racked my brain for somewhere else to go so our date wouldn't end. I suggested the mall, a restaurant, anywhere that was lit. She turned them all down. After a week working in the emergency room, the last thing she wanted was to be around more noise and people.

"Okay," I finally said. "Why don't we get a six-pack and hit a dirt road?"

"Yes!" she agreed. This was my kind of girl.

We drove around for the rest of the night talking.

᠊ᡒᡒᡒ

Janet and I were as compatible in marriage as we were online. She had lost a custody battle for her 11-year-old son, and we both missed the sound of children in the house. We fell into a routine of working, drinking beer, watching sports and going to bed.

My new wife was a blessing from the start. After about a year, she sent me to a urologist when she realized a problem I was having had medical implications. The lab work and MRI showed I had a benign brain tumor the size of a golf ball. The doctor said it had been there at least 10 years. The tumor had grown into my sinus cavity, messed up my adrenal gland and killed my testosterone level.

Treating it with medication didn't work, so in 2005, I had it surgically removed. I wondered if I would be a different person with my body more in balance.

But I was still me, character defects and all. I was a product of my environment, of a violent childhood and of 14 years working as a corrections officer in a violent environment.

I had tried to be the best person I could, but I had spent a lifetime being filled with negativity.

శ్రీశ్రీశ్రీ

When you work in a security environment, routine is paramount. Inmates can be unpredictable and dangerous, and it's important to stick to procedures designed for safety.

Inmates at the Department of Corrections were supposed to be transferred with their hands handcuffed behind their backs and the guard holding a six-foot tether. That way if the inmate tried to run away, the tether would serve as a leash and help the guard keep control. Procedure stated that officers were to hold the inmate by the cuffs as he walked, but some guards began ignoring the rule and only holding the end of the tether. New hires picked up on the slack practice.

With six feet of leeway, inmates quickly figured out

they could jerk around, head butt the guard and possibly escape.

I repeatedly told my supervisors how important it was to follow this procedure. I made sure my unit complied, but guards in other units were getting assaulted regularly during inmate transfers. My supervisors took no action on my complaints, and I began to feel like a kid whose parents were saying, "Just quit your whining." The more helpless I felt at work, the more my bitterness grew and the more I drank. I watched TV and drank. I worked in the yard and drank. I sat out on the porch and drank.

෴෴෴

While my relationship with Carys fell apart after Sharon and I divorced, I stayed close with Patrick. In 2009, he came over in early December to watch a football game and help us set up our Christmas tree. I'd never really enforced visitations with the kids because I didn't want to take them away from any activities they had going on. I was thrilled when Patrick said he'd be back on New Year's Day to watch the Rose Bowl, which the Ducks would be playing in.

Patrick didn't show up for Christmas, and he missed Janet's birthday the day after. I was seething during the kickoff to the Rose Bowl when there had been no sign of him. Little did I know that he was fed up with my drinking and had decided not to come around for a while.

As a young teenager Patrick was showing signs of

being mechanically inclined, so I'd put together $300 worth of tools into a starter toolset for his Christmas present. I stared at the toolset in my living room as my anger boiled over. He hadn't even allowed me an opportunity to give it to him!

I'd lost my license after a recent DUI, but I didn't care. I threw the toolbox into the passenger seat of my truck and sped over to Patrick's house. I was loaded with beer and fury and a deep hurt that my son, who I loved so much, hadn't even stopped by during the holidays.

The truck came to a jolting stop in Patrick's yard, and I stomped up to the front door with the toolbox. When he stepped out onto the porch, I slammed the box into his chest. Without a word, I stormed back to my truck and peeled around the corner to a neighborhood bar.

Patrick watched me drive away, his mouth open in surprise.

The beers at the bar calmed me down while I tried to figure out what I had done. Carys hadn't come over for Christmas in years, and I cherished the relationship that remained with Patrick. His absence crushed me.

Janet and I spent that evening in a familiar bar listening to live music. Sometime that evening I took a bathroom break, and when I turned around from the urinal, three guys I had never met were circled around me.

"You call him a n***er?" one of them asked, motioning to his friend and clearly trying to start something while the numbers were in his favor.

"Look, I'm not a racist. I happen to have African-

American friends. Why would I say something like that?"

As they considered what I said, I saw an opening. "If I even said anything like that, I'm sorry, okay? There's no reason for anyone to get upset. I'm sorry for anything that may have offended you."

I inched toward the door and kept talking, my humble words diffusing the situation. When I was close enough, I slipped out the door and sat down next to Janet.

"We've got to leave right now," I whispered into her ear. "Some guys were trying to start a fight with me in the bathroom."

We rushed out to the truck, and she cranked it up and slowly backed out of the parking space. Something snapped inside of me, and suddenly I was traveling in a vessel outside of my body and watching my hand punch through the truck's windshield as Janet looked on in horror. My hand was dripping with blood, but I couldn't feel it.

I threw open the truck door and strode back into the bar, scanning the room for the guys from the bathroom. They had split up, but I found one of them at a table with some other people.

"Hey," I said, nudging him with my bloody hand. "So, now what?"

He turned to look at me, his eyes blank. "Do I know you?" Without his posse, he wasn't interested in a fight.

Janet drove me home as quickly as she could.

࿐࿐࿐

LOSING THE FIGHT, WINNING THE BATTLE

Alcohol was like a fuel that magnified what's good in me to dangerous extremes. What had been compassion turned into a violent passion.

I had an ongoing battle with the city of Salem over a fence I had spent $5,000 erecting in my backyard. I had built it on an 18-inch retaining wall, and city officials said it was too high and needed to be torn down. My visits to city hall to understand why they were bringing this up four years after the fence was built were unfruitful. I took pictures and diagrams, but they refused to back down.

Finally, a city official clearly explained to me that there was no leeway in the rules. I can respect authority, and I understood that the fence was too high. But my anger wasn't so tempered.

My fury grew on the drive home, and when I pulled into the driveway, the Tasmanian devil version of myself hopped out of the cab of the truck. Fueled by a superhuman energy, I pulled all of the vinyl fence panels down with my bare hands in 15 minutes, rupturing a bicep in the process.

৵৵৵

I had developed a strong tolerance to alcohol, so even though I rarely felt drunk, I couldn't pass a Breathalyzer test.

I got my first DUI in 1993 on my way to a Quik-Mart a mile from my house to buy some chew. Because I had always tried to live in a lawful manner — I was a corrections officer, after all — I was infuriated when an officer pulled me over.

The officer had me walk the line in front of an apartment complex, and I pulled out my most obnoxious behavior for the sobriety test. I walked and talked with a drill sergeant cadence and put on such a show that the officer called for backup, and a crowd of apartment residents came out on their balconies to watch. I blew a .15, which is over the legal limit for blood-alcohol content, at the police station.

I got another DUI in 2008 when I rolled my truck on the way to a doctor's appointment. The back of the vehicle was filled with empty beer cans meant for recycling, and they scattered all over the road. I was taken to the ER and given a DUI.

On a cool fall afternoon in September of 2010, Janet and I headed to a bar to watch a football game. We left at halftime because it was such a rout, then went to sleep for five hours. I woke up at midnight, unable to doze off again, so I left Janet in bed and drove back to the bar to listen to a band. I drank four beers in three hours, and I got pulled over on my way home. I knew I was in trouble.

The officer said he pulled me over for an "evasive maneuver," and he drove me to the jail in Polk County. I refused to blow and asked to call my attorney.

The officer hustled me to a room with a telephone and literally tossed a phone book on the floor on the way out. I picked it up off the floor and dialed my lawyer's number.

The officer returned before I could make any

arrangements. "I've got an order of consent to draw blood," he told me. "We're going to the ER for the procedure. Let's go."

I held my composure. "You're not taking my blood," I said slowly. "This is America. We have rights here. You can't just take somebody off the street and force a blood draw."

"Sir, we have an order of consent signed by a judge. You need to come with me."

Adrenaline rushed through my veins like a freight train speeding through a tunnel, taking my last ounce of control with it.

"There's not enough of you here to take me down!" I screamed, morphing into the burly, hairy beast that had cowed me as a child. "I want my attorney. And if I can't talk to an attorney, let me talk to my wife!"

The hums and beeps of the police radio filled the room as the officer called for backup. I continued ranting until someone who knew my wife would be working in the ER that night got her on the phone. She confirmed that the blood draw was authorized.

My indignation deflated, and I dutifully followed the officer through arraignment and then to my jail cell. For the first time, I was seeing the inside of a cell as an inmate rather than as the guard locking a prisoner inside. The cell was rank and damp, and I felt like I was sitting at the bottom of a well.

Even though I drank only four beers over a couple of hours at the bar, I had been drinking earlier that day, and I knew my blood level was going to come up over the legal amount.

My 36 hours in that jail cell were my rock bottom. Within a week, I was enrolled in a three-week inpatient treatment program.

ॐॐॐ

This wasn't my first time in treatment, but it was the first time I followed through with the 12 steps of Alcoholics Anonymous. The third step requires you to offer yourself to God. I was ready.

I spoke to God in my den, a dark room with no windows. I turned out the lights because I was looking for the light of the Holy Spirit that I could *sense*, not see. I knelt down on one knee because in my mind Jesus Christ is the Lord, and I wanted to kneel as a knight would to a lord. When my knee touched the ground, I asked God to forgive me for all of the wrong things I had done, including the things I didn't even know I had done. It wasn't important to list every single thing. God knew.

In the silence, I just listened, for anything. I closed my eyes and crossed my arms over my knee, and soon I saw a flicker of light. It got brighter, and I knew it was the light of hope, signifying God's promise that he loves me and had plans for my future. That light melted my heart and allowed me to forgive myself for everything I had done. The buzzing inside my head, the car horns, the city sounds, the people talking, all went silent. The room was still and serene.

LOSING THE FIGHT, WINNING THE BATTLE

The tears came next, flowing down my face. The wet tracks that they left washed my soul.

ॐॐॐ

I've changed what fills me up every day. My radio station is tuned to Christian music. The bookshelves in my den are lined with several versions of the Bible, study books and Christian commentaries. I wear a cross around my neck, which symbolizes the new covenant between God and me. When I was baptized, I rose out of that water as a new person.

Every day, I study the Bible for at least 30 minutes. I read in my den, where the walls are covered with plaques and awards I've won for good things I've done at work. But they mean nothing. I tarnished my life with poor choices, and now I'm trying to live the way God wants me to.

There is one award, however, that holds a lifetime of meaning for me. My son gave it to me.

Missing my children broke me. Even though I still don't have my kids living with me, I have God's family now at Relevant Life Church, where Janet and I are members. Everyone there is a brother and a sister to me. That's taken the pressure off Patrick, who has stayed in my life.

But Patrick made sure to come over recently for one of the most important milestone days of my life.

"Dad," he said, "I got you something."

UNDEFEATED

What passed between us was so simple, yet so complex. He opened his palm to show me a royal purple coin, emblazoned with "1" to signify my year of sobriety.

"I'm proud of you," he said softly.

I'd never seen anything like this medallion. It glinted in the light, reflecting the joy that poured from my soul. I bawled like a baby.

I wish I could have been a better influence on Patrick's life. I still have a long way to go. But every day is a step toward God and the promises and plans he has for my life. My story is just beginning.

CONCLUSION

When I became a pastor, my desire was to change the world. My hope was to see people suffering from discouragement find encouragement, those bound by addictions set free, the hopeless find hope, those feeling defeated come out UNDEFEATED! As I read this book, I see that passion being fulfilled. I see the relevant God that I serve become relevant to every person, in every situation and through all circumstances, regardless of their background. At Relevant Life Church, we are not content with our past victories; we are spurred to believe that many more can occur.

Every time we see another changed life, it increases our awareness that God really loves people, and he is actively seeking to change lives. Think about it: How did you get this book? We believe you read this book because God brought it to you seeking to reveal his love to you. Whether you are male or female, young or old, we believe God came to save you. He came to save us. Jesus Christ came to give each person abundant, vibrant and RELEVANT life.

Do you question if such radical change is possible? It seems too good to be true, doesn't it? Each of us at Relevant Life Church warmly invites you to come and check out our church family. Freely ask questions, examine our statements, see if we're "for real" and, if you choose, journey with us at whatever pace you are comfortable. You will find that we are far from perfect. Our scars and sometimes open wounds are still healing, but we want you to know God is still completing the process of authentic life change in us. We still make mistakes throughout our journey, like everyone will. Therefore, we acknowledge our continued need for each other's forgiveness and support. We need the love of God just as much now as we did the day before we met him.

If you are unable to be with us, yet you desire to experience such a life change, here are some basic thoughts to consider. If you choose, at the end of this conclusion, you can pray the suggested prayer and experience the beginning stages of authentic life change, similar to those you have read about.

How does this change occur?

Recognize that Jesus is God's Son and that he died on a cross to pay for everyone's wrongdoings.

Recognize that what you're doing isn't working. Accept the fact that Jesus desires to forgive you for your bad decisions and selfish motives. Realize that without this forgiveness, you will continue a life separated from God and his amazing love. In the Bible, the book of Romans, chapter 6, verse 23 reads, "The result of sin (seeking our way rather than God's way) is death, but the gift that God freely gives is everlasting life found in Jesus Christ."

Believe in your heart that God passionately loves you and wants to give you a new heart. Ezekiel 11:19 reads, "I will give them singleness of heart and put a new spirit within them. I will take away their stony, stubborn heart and give them a tender, responsive heart" (NLT).

Believe in your heart that "if you confess with your mouth that Jesus is Lord and believe in your heart that God raised him from the dead, you will be saved" (Romans 10:9 NLT).

Believe in your heart that because Jesus paid for your failure and wrong motives, and because you asked him to forgive you, he has filled your new heart with his life in such a way that he transforms you from the inside out. Second Corinthians 5:17 reads, "When someone becomes a Christian, he becomes a brand-new person inside. He is not the same anymore. A new life has begun!"

Why not pray now?

Lord Jesus, if I've learned one thing in my journey, it's that you are God and I am not. My choices have not resulted in the happiness I hoped they would bring. Not only have I experienced pain, I've also caused it. I know I am separated from you, but I want that to change. I am sorry for the choices I've made that have hurt me and others, and I need your forgiveness. I believe your death paid for my sins, and you are now alive to change me from the inside out. Would you please do that now? I ask you to come and live in me so that I can sense you are here with me. Thank you for hearing me and changing me. Now please help me know when you are talking to me, so I can cooperate with your efforts to change me. Amen.

UNDEFEATED

Relevant Life Church's unfolding story of God's love is still being written ... and your name is in it.

I hope to see you this Sunday!

Kevin Reich, Lead Pastor
Relevant Life Church

We would love for you to join us at
Relevant Life Church!

We meet Sunday mornings at 8:30 and 11 a.m. at
1090 Fairview Avenue SE, Salem, OR 97302.

Fairview Ave SE

Summer St SE

Bluff Ave SE

12th St SE

Please call us at 503.364.7759 for directions, or
contact us at www.relevantlifechurch.net.
There's something for every age!

For more information on reaching your city with
stories from your church, please contact
Good Catch Publishing at
www.goodcatchpublishing.com

GOOD CATCH
PUBLISHING

Did one of these stories touch you?
Did one of these real people move you to tears?
Tell us (and them) about it on our reader blog at
www.goodcatchpublishing.blogspot.com.